VIOLENT
DEATH
IN THE CITY

This volume is published as part of a long-standing cooperative program between Harvard University Press and the Commonwealth Fund, a philanthropic foundation, to encourage the publication of significant scholarly books in medicine and health.

VIOLENT
DEATH
IN THE CITY

SUICIDE, ACCIDENT, AND MURDER
IN NINETEENTH-CENTURY
PHILADELPHIA

Roger Lane

A Commonwealth Fund Book

Harvard University Press
Cambridge, Massachusetts
and London, England
1979

Library of Congress Cataloging in Publication Data
Lane, Roger.
    Violent death in the city.

    "A Commonwealth Fund book."
    Includes bibliographical references and index.
    1. Violence—Pennsylvania—Philadelphia—History—
19th century.   2. Violent deaths—Pennsylvania—Phila-
delphia—History—19th century.   3. Philadelphia—
Social conditions.   I. Title.
HN80.P5L36   301.6'33'0974811   79-11836
ISBN 0-674-93946-8

To Eileen Brenda O'Connor Lewis

PREFACE

This short book is the product of my long inter-
est in the controversy surrounding the issues of public order and
social control in cities. The pursuit of this interest, while originally stimulated by the ill-informed and often racist "law and
order" debates of the 1960s and 1970s, has led to research in the
often simpler patterns of urban development that marked the
previous century. The trail has been as often obscured as illumi-
nated by numbers; the official statistics of pathological behavior, in particular, are easily subject to naive abuse. Much of the
argument here, too, is based upon numbers, but their use has
deliberately been kept simple. There is more emphasis upon the
way in which official figures were recorded and the reality behind them than upon statistical manipulation of these figures as
received. No operation performed has been more complicated
than the basic four, and tests for significance have been avoided
entirely. Although the materials are here for aficionados to pursue at greater length, no single table or set of figures is critical to
the argument as a whole. My intention is to make the findings
fully accessible to readers who are uncomfortable in the presence of statistical data.

In terms of this intention, the title suggests three further considerations. First, the study is confined to one city, but it might
as well have been any other, and it is hoped that the conclusions

will apply equally elsewhere. The choice of Philadelphia is perfectly defensible in terms of its strong and early commitment to industrialism, the state of its records, and the richness of the historical literature devoted to it; in fact it was chosen largely because I have lived in or near it for the past fifteen years. Second, the terminal dates were dictated more by necessity than by design; the absence of certain critical records before the late 1830s prevented studying the nineteenth century as a whole, and thus only the sixty-three years from 1839 to 1901 are covered. Last, as the introduction explains, my interest is not in death but in the life of the past, with the records of mortality used simply as clues to living behavior.

Portions of the introduction first appeared in my article "Crime and the Industrial Revolution: British and American Views," *Journal of Social History* (Fall 1974), and are reprinted with permission. In the course of gathering and interpreting the material for subsequent chapters I have acquired a number of debts. For this as well as my earlier work, much inspiration, however indirect, was provided by Oscar Handlin. A grant from the National Endowment for the Humanities gave me time to reflect; the Haverford College Faculty Research Fund and the Commonwealth Fund helped me obtain much-needed assistance. Michael Magaril, Mitchell Olney, Anne Orens, and Paul Perkal, along with Joshua Kosman and Deborah Perloe for the computerized homicide series especially, often contributed suggestions as well as raw materials. The staffs of the Haverford College Library, of the Philadelphia City Records Department, and of the Municipal Archives were consistently patient with everyone. Henry Williams of the Philadelphia Social History Project, which is directed by Theodore Hershberg, was a frequent source of arcane statistical data. Harold Cox contributed some of his immense knowledge of nineteenth-century railroading; Doctors Robert Catherman, Robert Katz, and Robert Siegel of the Philadelphia Medical Examiner's Office, and Dr. Christopher Johnson, supplied expertise about medical practice past and present. Frank Hartleroad, James Mohr, and Charles Silberman all allowed access to their research prior to publication. The manuscript was criticized, in whole or in part, by Richard

Jensen, Eric Monkkonen, Elizabeth Pleck, Marc Ross, and two scholars whose work is crucial to its argument, Marvin Wolfgang and Martin Gold; all of their suggestions were perceptive, and some were incorporated. Aida Donald of Harvard University Press was encouraging at a critical early stage. Margaret Anderson edited the final draft with care and intelligence. Adeline Taraborelli did her usual thorough job of typing the manuscript. And my wife, Marjorie Merklin, provided many of the services mentioned above and more.

CONTENTS

TABLES

CHAPTER 1

INTRODUCTION

Much of the material in these pages is about death, but the real subject is life, the living behavior of thousands of largely anonymous Philadelphians during most of the nineteenth century, the years 1839 to 1901. Of many of these people, the only record that remains is the final entry: perhaps a story in the paper, more surely a brief notation by some agent of the state of information incident to the way in which they died. The manner of dying is, however, often a reflection of the manner of living, and these largely unexplored records may provide much new information about the changing conditions of ordinary life. They are used here to suggest a reexamination of the link between growth and disorder, or violence, two themes that have dominated the traditional history and sociology of American cities in that period. It is the purpose of this book first to establish the usefulness of the indices of suicide, accident, and homicide as measures of personal behavior, especially violence, and then to indicate the relative impact of population growth and other influences on that behavior.

The city of Philadelphia was once the largest in the United States and currently ranks fourth; between 1840 and 1900, it slipped from second to third. But despite this relative retrogression, growth of several kinds remains a natural focus for study. The period was one of the most important in urban history everywhere, encompassing the many changes defined collectively as the "industrial revolution." Philadelphia's experience was in many respects typical. Already at the beginning a financial, commercial, and hand-manufacturing center, by century's end the city had moved into the era of steam and even electric power with a strong and highly diverse industrial base. Its population, starting at a quarter of a million in 1840, reached six times that in 1900. The life of its people was increasingly shaped by larger and more complex institutions, governing work, communications, and related activities. All of these developments affected the behavior of Philadelphia's residents. Some of them still do, for in certain respects the problem of violence in the twentieth-century city may be related to patterns that originated in the nineteenth.

Before establishing and interpreting these patterns, however, it is necessary to outline two alternative versions of the link between growth and disorder, one of them constructed by an older generation of sociologists, one by the current generation of historians.

The impact of cities on the lives of those who experienced the time of their greatest growth was long a subject of popular concern, even before it became a matter for scholarly analysis. Scholarship in general is most influential when it serves to footnote the conventional wisdom, and in this case that alliance has proved especially strong. The major accomplishment of classical urban sociology, best defined by the "Chicago School" of the 1920s and thereafter, was to provide a theoretical framework for political and intellectual distrust of the city, shored up with documentation of the most impressive sort.

The antiurban tradition in American politics needs little elaboration. Thomas Jefferson is the most protean as well as the most quoted of the Founding Fathers, but on this issue his most famous quotation—"The mobs of great cities, add just so much to the support of pure government, as sores do to the strength of the human body"—is not balanced by any other. While the specific agrarian-yeoman ideology that inspired such sentiments has faded, it remains true that no American president since has been identified as a spokesman for the urban way of life, and an analysis of nearly two centuries of campaign rhetoric might suggest that as a people we moved from farm to suburb without any intervening step.

The historic hostility of intellectuals toward the city is almost equally familiar, if somewhat more complicated. None would deny that the city is essential to high culture or to certain kinds of personal freedom. But until quite recently most of the creators and conservators of culture have spoken not so much for culture itself as for the cultured class. And for the cultured class, the city's attractions were overbalanced by poverty and disorder and compounded by noise, dirt, and the often alien character of the residents.[1]

The new science of sociology, in the nineteenth and early twentieth centuries, was well designed to reinforce these attitudes. The ancient Western nostalgia for a simpler past was revivified in the Romantic Era. Concern about the transition from *Gemeinschaft* to *Gesellschaft* was natural to those nineteenth-century intellectuals who perceived themselves as having lived through it. The first scholarly formulation of this concern, by Ferdinand Tönnies, was unabashedly romantic in tone. Later this notion was given more nearly objective formulation by Max Weber and in different fashion by Emile Durkheim, but much the same point was made. It was still impossible, in moral terms, to regard the transition from simple to complex, from small to large, from village to city, as anything but descent.

It is appropriate that urban sociology, in particular, should have received its fullest formulation in America and specifically in Chicago. The antiurban tradition was especially strong in this country, and nowhere was growth more dramatic. The concern created by this conjunction was further heightened by a third characteristic, the reforming impulse, which early in the twentieth century prompted, among other things, investigation of the many ills of urban society in order to alleviate them. By the 1920s, all of these elements combined to help create perhaps the most influential "school" of social scientists in our history, the sociologists led by professors Ernest Burgess and Robert E. Park of the University of Chicago.

The school made contributions of several sorts, but for present purposes the most important was its analysis of what its members were not afraid to call the "character" of people in cities.[2] By their nature, great cities, the followers of Park and Burgess agreed, presented enormous problems of social control. The transition from community to metropolis was marked by the loss of "primary relationships," close, fully personal contacts as between neighboring families, in favor of "secondary relationships," relatively impersonal and specialized contacts, as between customer and clerk. The inculcation of social and personal morality, the key to social order, was heavily handicapped by the impersonality of communication in big urban centers, the fleeting and often wholly exploitative nature of most contacts among their inhabitants. Social values are best taught in primary groups, such as the family and the village church; the secondary institutions, police, courts, and schools, which replaced some of their functions in the city could not fully keep up. The result was an inevitable tendency toward disintegration of the social order, and indeed of the "character" of those who composed the society. As city life undermined inherited tradition and freed people of constraint, so "urban expansion is accompanied by excessive increases in disease, crime, disorder, vice, insanity, and suicide, rough indices of social disorganization."[3]

Burgess's characterization of urban pathology and disorder came well furnished with apparently solid fact. Statistics could be gathered that contrasted rural and urban places, sometimes individual urban places over time, and showed that criminal arrests for morals offenses, or divorce actions, or insanity commitments, were all proportionately more common in big places than in small ones. Although these studies typically did not reconstruct the actual history of any given city in detail, they implied a history for all. The transition from small to large, from simple to complex, from orderly to disorderly conditions and behavior, was also the transition from an idealized earlier republic to the contemporary scene. The sociologists in short could prove what Americans knew already: that there was a price for growth in Chicago or Philadelphia, a price measured in terms of individually and socially pathological behavior, perhaps above all in terms of violence.[4]

      During the period in which the Chicago School first flourished, there was virtually no dissent from the assumptions on which it was based. Neither the interest nor the materials necessary for a critique were available until recently. And while some scholars have suggested doubts, and historians have constructed a somewhat different version of social order in nineteenth-century cities, the Chicago framework for understanding changes in personal behavior still stands high, its foundations undermined but with no comprehensive alternative in sight.

Cities throughout the nineteenth century were powerfully attractive in the root sense of that word, but their attractions were elemental and immediate, never clothed in ideology. Millions of people came for concrete reasons, driven from elsewhere, seeking variety or opportunity or escape. Few came persuaded by anything but individual experience that city life was inherently superior.

There were champions of urban progress, but they spoke generally not for all cities but for one. The *Annual Addresses* of the mayors of any large city collectively record proud accomplishments ranging from increases in the mileage of gas mains and street railways to sheer population growth. But like the advertisements of local boosters and realtors, the rhetoric of local politicians was tainted by interest. And its emphasis on things material was not designed to appeal to those few intellectuals who chose, in entirely different fashion, to celebrate life in the city. With notable exceptions, such as Carl Sandburg and Walt Whitman, these intellectuals celebrated an urbanity as little touched as possible by industrial technology and change. Their only common ground with the boosters was the fact that they too were partisans of particular places, Cambridge or Brooklyn or Greenwich Village, but never Birmingham or Cleveland.

Professional historians as a group, meanwhile, contributed very little to urban studies. In the early twentieth century, having recently returned from searching for democracy in the forests of pre-Christian Germany, most were engaged in the same quest in the forests of frontier Wisconsin. Life in the city was systematically ignored; the 1950 edition of the most influential of American history texts, the massive two-volume survey by Morison and Commager, contains just one index item under "city" and three under "urbanization," one of these a reference to growing crime rates.[5] The few who did pioneer in the history of cities during the twenties, thirties, and forties tended a little uneasily to accept and thus bolster the framework supplied by the sociologists. Although insisting on the importance of their subject, they conceded the corrosive effect of the urban environment upon the character and behavior of the masses.[6]

Recent interest in urban studies among historians as well as other scholars has, however, raised some questions about the Chicago hypothesis. One set of questions relates to the use of criminal statistics as evidence for "real" pathological behavior. Both sociologists and historians have grown more sophisticated in their approach to these figures, and while agreeing that they do measure something, they are not so confident that they measure what they are supposed to.[7] Rising arrests for drunkenness, for example, may indicate an increase in drunkenness, but it is more likely, in the context of the nineteenth-century city, that they indicate higher standards of public behavior enforced by growing numbers of professional police.[8] Similarly the figures for divorce may reflect regularization, legitimization, and recording of the informal practice of desertion. Upon examination, much of the apparently hardest evidence for disorganization and pathology in the nineteenth century is at best inconclusive and may sometimes indicate the very reverse of what was earlier alleged.

Historians, meanwhile, have at least partly challenged the idea that disorder was in any simple way a function of growth over time. It is characteristic of the discipline that several scholars have separately described particular places and periods, but a collective version of events may be drawn from these individual accounts. And while such a composite owes something to the histories of several major eastern centers, and applies at least in part to all, it perhaps best fits the city of Philadelphia.[9]

Relatively little has been written about the time between the American Revolution and the 1830s. But in the version offered by modern histories, it appears to have been a relatively peaceful time in which politics was the prerogative of the privileged, and population growth, however rapid, did not outrun the city's capacity to absorb it. Political and social problems erupted rather in the decades just before the Civil War.

That was a period of the most headlong demographic growth in the history of all American cities, and particularly in Philadelphia. The newcomers, mostly Irish and German immigrants, were generally poorer than more established citizens, desperately so during and just after the potato famines of the "Hungry Forties." They competed with each other and with the long-established free black population for jobs at the bottom of the system. They competed, further, in a changing economy. The old economic order, based on skilled hand manufacture, finance, and commerce, did not provide much employment for large numbers of the wholly unskilled. But this new labor pool combined with technological and organizational developments to enable the factory system to move from the fringes to the center of the city's economy, upsetting old arrangements while creating new ones. And all the time the looming threat of civil war heightened political tensions locally as well as nationally, providing additional reasons for the already evident hostilities among groups.

The constant pouring of new immigrants into this confused situation made riotous conflict likely, and inadequate local institutions made it inevitable. The ancient system of watch and constables, sometimes backed by the sheriff's posse and ultimately by the militia, was at best an ineffective means of keeping order. In Philadelphia official weakness was exacerbated by unrealistic political boundaries. The official city was a narrow strip between the Delaware and Schuylkill rivers, squeezed among several other jurisdictions within the county, each with its own police and courts. No power, apparently, could curb the growth of youth gangs which, often allied with firemen organized along the same neighborhood and ethnic lines, terrorized honest citizens while battling with each other. These young men figured in most local conflicts, whether sparked initially by labor trouble, racial hatred, or ethnic jealousy. Sometimes their chronic rioting became acute, all authority was defied, and nothing short of military force was capable of stopping them.

These conditions, growing through the 1840s and 1850s, served at least to unite the city's elite. Whatever their differences, established Philadelphians could not tolerate the recurrent smell of smoke and threat of anarchy. In 1854, the county was consolidated into a single city under one government, largely to enable the creation of a single professional police force, which was soon armed to deal with ruffians. On another level, stronger citywide political organizations absorbed and in some sense legitimized many tensions that before had erupted physically. The Civil War, once burst, blew away some others. The rest of the century then passed in comparative peace. The city, if not governed wisely or well, was at least governed, under effectively one-party rule, and local authority was never again seriously threatened by armed mobs of young residents.[10]

A composite historical picture such as this contradicts the implicit view of the Chicago sociologists at two points. It argues first that violent disorder is and was not a function simply of size and impersonality, since the small city of the 1840s and 1850s was more riotous than the metropolis of the 1890s. And further, it is less fatalistic about mechanisms of control; secondary institutions, politically administered, from party organizations to the police force, may make a significant difference in the behavior of belligerent elements in the population.

This version of events is convincing so far as it goes, but still it is not a full alternative to the view posited by the Chicago group. The historians have not challenged the sociologists directly, simply because they are dealing with different sorts of behavior. Historians have long been interested in collective violence. Much of the recent focus upon urban history has resulted from a shift in interest down and away from the activities of elite groups and toward those of the less articulate; in terms of violence this has involved a shift from studying international or civil warfare to studying local riot, rout, and tumult. But collective behavior of this sort indicates relatively little about the behavior of the individuals involved. And in this case small-scale disturbances may not be an appropriate measure of disorder, since much recent work has stressed the limited, purposeful, and rational nature of mob actions once thought mindless.[11] Much of what seemed anarchy to Philadelphia's leadership may in fact have been purposeful violence sanctioned by large numbers of citizens, designed to win or protect place and position. The passing of riot as a normal form of political expression simply means, to the historians, that better alternatives were developed and implies nothing about the personal behavior, the socialization, certainly not the improved "character" of potential rioters.

In fact, there is now no satisfactory explanation or measure of the impact of urban development on the ordinary behavior of the populace. While the historians' version seems sound, it is neither comprehensive nor fully relevant. The Chicago version, while both comprehensive and relevant, can no longer be considered fully sound. The increasing use of statistical series by students of urban history has succeeded in weakening the old argument about urban pathology but has not generally been directed at constructing another. And so, partly by default, the old framework remains.

But the issues that Park, Burgess, Wirth, and their followers sought to clarify remain important ones. And the use of numbers to illumine them, however crudely done, was not in itself wrongheaded. Apparently impersonal data can be made to reveal much about the most personal matters, as historians of the family, among others, have shown. And if the more neutral term "behavior" is substituted for "character," and better indices for the suspect statistics of jails, courts, and asylums, it is possible to test propositions very like those posited by the Chicagoans.

My purpose is to establish and partially interpret a set of hard indices that have not been used in this way before. If violence is defined as physically reckless, aggressive, or destructive behav-

ior, then surely suicide, accident, and homicide are all manifestations of violence. The number of deaths from these causes is a
figure available for virtually every major Western city in the
later nineteenth century.[12] Although the process of collection
was often flawed, the records of mortality are superior to those
of criminality and other forms of deviance, in that virtually all
violent deaths of adults were officially registered in some fashion, and it may be assumed that few persons were so registered
more than once. It is true that individual cases vary in import,
that the statistics are often misleading without painstaking verification, and that they may seem meaningless without analysis.
But for a large population, with the precautions described in the
text and appendixes, such figures may be used as a uniquely
important source of social history.

The raw data for Philadelphia, the basis for much of what
follows, are given in Table 1. (For homicides, see the rather different sort of enumeration in Table 8 and Table 13.) As these
numbers are analyzed, the separate discussions of suicide, accident, and homicide should provide some insight into a number
of matters, ranging from the operations of the criminal justice
system to the changing technology of cooking. But the ultimate
focus is on those concerns that the sociologists first elaborated:
the impact of population growth and new economic organization, of the substitution of large for small units of work and of
formal for informal means of schooling. The conclusion will
sum up and indicate the meaning of all the numbers combined.
In offering a different interpretation of the changing level of urban violence and of the impact of the industrial city on those
who lived through its development, it may also help illumine
the condition of those who are now living through its decline.

Table 1. Philadelphia's population and number of deaths from suicide, casualties, burns and scalds, and drownings, 1839-1901.

Year	Population (in 1,000s)	Cause of Death			
		Suicide	Cas.	B&S	Drownings
1839	250	16	25	16	40
1840	258	14	27	21	54
1841	270	16	35	17	46
1842	284	12	26	16	49
1843	297	12	27	14	49
1844	311	10	38	32	47
1845	325	19	31	31	45
1846	341	5	36	25	46
1847	357	8	50	29	59
1848	374	17	47	27	65
1849	392	9	64	29	60
1850	409	20	70	48	96
1851	422	14	46	54	63
1852	436	14	75	27	64
1853	450	14	105	38	73
1854	464	13	113	40	110
1855	479	26	131	36	101
1856	495	34	149	58	103
1857	511	32	108	33	105
1858	527	21	142	46	102
1859	544	21	140	56	92
1860	565	17	123	30	117
1861	578	31	103	81	99
1862	587	14	135	81	135
1863	598	24	120	85	131
1864	608	20	178	89	133
1865	619	31	152	68	163
1866	630	44	168	45	137
1867	641	35	172	61	125
1868	652	29	177	63	120
1869	662	45	181	68	103
1870	674	25	191	58	149
1871	691	41	203	90	113
1872	709	48	217	82	114
1873	726	47	218	88	130
1874	743	59	190	67	131
1875	760	68	217	81	119

(cont.)

Table 1.   *(cont.)*

Year	Population (in 1,000s)	Cause of Death			
		Suicide	Cas.	B&S	Drownings
1876	778	60	225	68	111
1877	795	59	190	59	127
1878	812	40	146	68	129
1879	830	51	174	55	105
1880	847	68	226	100	115
1881	868	62	—	—	—
1882	886	77	316	77	111
1883	907	95	305	71	96
1884	927	89	340	68	93
1885	949	78	327	82	110
1886	971	90	323	89	100
1887	994	88	351	73	86
1888	1,017	94	378	69	87
1889	1,040	104	355	95	107
1890	1,046	80	421	85	97
1891	1,068	108	421	95	103
1892	1,092	102	488	133	96
1893	1,116	123	533	75	87
1894	1,139	134	542	93	86
1895	1,164	105	548	119	87
1896	1,189	136	496	137	88
1897	1,214	143	433	116	93
1898	1,240	165	467	166	100
1899	1,266	160	473	149	93
1900	1,294	153	511	149	99
1901	1,323	160	501	144	118

Source: See appendix A.

CHAPTER 2

SUICIDE

The relations of suicide to certain states of social environment are as direct and constant as its relations to facts of a biological and physical character.

Emile Durkheim, *Suicide*

Of all the indices of violent death, the one for suicide is the most problematic, the most controversial, and the best place to begin. The academic subindustry that deals with the topic is large enough to warrant its own title, suicidology, and more than broad enough to include several warring schools. Most of the problems, fortunately, lie outside the scope of this book. Suicide as a unique act committed by a particular person may be conceived of as having as many meanings as the number of human beings affected, and the range of psychological possibilities is nearly as wide. But for students of society, who have traditionally focused on the comparative rates of self-destruction among various subgroups, such as rich and poor, the number of explanations has never been large. Especially among those concerned not merely with static frequencies but with social change, the list is as simple as it is short, involving relatively uncomplicated correlations with the business cycle, the political situation, and various other indices of social health or pathology.

The materials from nineteenth-century Philadelphia do bear on these traditional arguments and concerns. They also suggest others of a qualitatively different sort. But the first task is, or should be, the difficult one of establishing the data. The psychologist starts with a single, starkly undeniable event, but a study such as this can never take for granted that its statistical raw material reflects reality in the same direct fashion. Before the task of interpretation can begin, it is necessary to show that the figures are strong enough to bear the weight assigned.

> Accidentally shot while cleaning the muzzle of the gun with his tongue.
>
> Legendary West of Ireland inquest verdict

The official statistics for suicide in nineteenth-century Philadelphia, as compiled by the health office from certificates filed by the coroner, show the simplest pattern of any of the indices of violence. If the sixty-three years from 1839 through 1901 are divided into nine seven-year intervals, the resulting table shows little progressive change until about 1870, when the slope rises dramatically to the end of the century.[1]

The figures are of course inaccurate, undercounted, as are all official suicide statistics; no one knows or ever has known how many people deliberately kill themselves in a given year. But such figures, whatever their other uses, indicate something about the social experience and expectations of the society that generates them. And those for Philadelphia, when tested, yield something stronger than that. The issue is not really one of absolute but of relative accuracy, not of the "true" rate but of the direction of that rate, up or down. There is always the possibility that the official statistics of suicide are so far removed from reality as to be utterly misleading guides to that reality, that massive numbers either escaped diagnosis or were knowingly hidden by physicians and coroners under wholly unrelated labels, such as "apoplexy" or "heart disease." But even if that is the case, the figures are no more unreal than those of the present era; the crude annual rate for the end of the nineteenth century, 12.2 per 100,000, is almost identical to the modern one, and if standardized by age it is slightly higher.[2] In short the figures are

Table 2. Crude average annual suicide rates per 100,000 population by period, 1839-1901.

Years	Average rate	Years	Average rate
1839-1845	5.0	1867-1873	5.6
1846-1852	3.2[1]	1874-1880	7.0
1853-1859	4.8	1881-1887	9.0
1860-1867	4.3	1888-1894	10.0
		1895-1901	11.8

Source: See appendix A.
1. See note 5 to this chapter for explanation of this apparent anomaly.

at worst no worse than those on which all modern studies have been based, and in this respect they have been more thoroughly examined than any.[3]

> Verdict in accordance with the facts above.
> Traditional last line in newspaper
> suicide reports

Nothing in the history of the institution of the coroner's jury suggests that it is wise to believe in suicide verdicts without careful scrutiny.[4] A sin for Christians since the time of Augustine, suicide was also a crime at common law; a peculiar legal "catch-22" has led, on rare occasions, to official prosecutions for failed attempts. In some cases the pressure to bring a more seemly verdict must have conquered jurors' judgments. And in the years for which a crosscheck is possible, there are rare instances in which the verdict itself was circumvented in the registration process, as when "suicide—laudanum" was rendered simply "laudanum." But assuming that this time-honored device—the attribution of cause without motive, as in "gunshot wound" or "suffocation by illuminating gas"—was the one normally employed, it is possible at least to set quantitative limits to the problem.

The coroner himself had no vested financial or other interest in concealing suicides, barring some form of bribery by family or friends; indeed, his concern was to patrol the boundaries of his jurisdiction, finding warrant whenever possible for "suspicion" in cases of doubt. Sometimes, in fact, coroners publicly reprimanded doctors for failing to report suicides or otherwise follow proper procedures. But the remarkably consistent slope of the suicide rate suggests, with two possible early exceptions, that to the extent that official policy rather than objective circumstance governed the choice of verdict (or indeed the decision to submit certain cases to inquest verdicts at all), the policy was set by the city's medical fraternity rather than by its coroners.[5] The coroners, mostly laymen, succeeded each other too rapidly to design and transmit any coherent set of hidden rules. All of them, even the physicians who filled the office, employed medical doctors to provide the testimony and authority needed for guiding jurors. Originally called on a case-by-case basis, with a few names constantly recurring, these coroner's physicians were officially put on the staff in the 1870s. Even then they remained doctors, with private practice along with their government position. They were very much in the public eye, required to argue as well as consult with their peers in difficult cases, more generally to act as members of a professional subculture with its own standards. Indeed in certain situations, such as a physician's extreme negligence or failure to follow the dictates of the Registration Act and the health codes, it was the coroner's office that invoked the sanctions for those standards, through actions of censure by the juries. The keepers of burial grounds, themselves closely supervised by the health office, were the ultimate filters for the system and reported to the coroner egregious cases of misrepresentation of the cause of death.[6]

Under these arrangements, policed by a combination of mild coercion and mutual consent, there were—barring the extreme and perhaps risky "apoplexy" alternative—two sorts of possible cover-up: those in which a doctor or other witnesses misrepresented the facts in a suspicious case and those in which the coroner himself knowingly signed a false certificate. In these cases the problem may be reduced to a kind of *ex post facto* detective work, a search, literally, for hidden bodies, in categories that might conceal unhallowed deaths.

The key period here is 1870 to 1900. Between those dates the real break occurred, beginning the sharp upward slope that must be explained in terms of real changes either in the incidence of suicide or in the policy governing reportage. Between 1868-1872 and 1899-1901 the age-standardized aggregate rate more than doubled, in fact, moving from 5.8 per 100,000 to 12.2.[7] And there is enough recorded information to suggest the degree to which these official figures reflect a parallel change in the real world.

Five suspicious "accident" categories are immediately apparent: "gunshot wounds," "poisoning," "strangulation," "suffocation" (of adults), and "unknown causes." These are listed in Table 3. None of these categories shows the characteristics necessary to explain the dramatic rise in the suicide figures. The case of "unknown" causes is treated at length in chapter 5; for the present it is enough to note that virtually none of them could reasonably be regarded as suicides. Of those remaining, only gunshot wounds and strangulation were proportionately greater during the first period than during the second, as was generally true for accidents that did not involve complex technology. But both categories are absolutely far too small to account for the difference in suicide rates; even assuming that only the 1870 figures are undercounted, it would require over a hundred additional suicides to cancel the increase. There are only two accident categories large enough to have hidden that many cases: "casualties," which includes falls from buildings and windows, and "drownings" (see Table 1).

Table 3. Deaths in "suspicious" categories: 5- and 3-year totals and crude average annual rates per 100,000 population, 1868-1872 and 1899-1901.

Years	Gunshot No./rate	Poison No./rate	Strang. No./rate	Suffoc. No./rate	Unknown No./rate
1868-1872	58/1.8	59/1.7	27/0.8	49/1.4	596/17.7
1899-1901	27/0.7	100/2.6	9/0.2	61/1.6	3/0.0

Source: See appendix A.

Of the two, "casualties" is the least likely, beginning with the fact that there were proportionately as many of them around 1900 as around 1870. Moreover, the most obvious sort of casualty suicide—falls from high places—could not have been very common in either period; an educated estimate (see the discussion of accidents in chapter 3) is that after eliminating job-related falls, there were no more than ten or a dozen each year. Several of these typically were of boys picking cherries from trees; most adults who died from falls not related to their jobs were elderly people who slipped on pavements or down stairwells, neither of which is a reliable means of self-destruction. Other sorts of casualties may be discounted similarly; the incidence of most types was growing rather than declining with the increase in lethal technological hazards. And while the category is a large one, it does not contain much to indicate suicide. Attorneys for the great railroads, perhaps readers of Trollope or Tolstoy, sometimes argued that the mounting number of fatalities on the tracks was due in significant part to suicidal pedestrians, but they never convinced inquest juries.[8] For the last eighteen years of the century, either the coroner or the health officer usually reported the specific means employed in suicide cases.[9] The official list of methods of self-destruction counts only about 3 percent as people jumping from heights, throwing themselves in front of trains, or otherwise incurring miscellaneous external injuries. Whatever the real incidence of suicidal casualties, Philadelphians did not believe, or were not told, that the despondent commonly turned to such untidy measures.

> As watchman Miles of the Franklin Sugar Refinery was making his rounds at the foot of Bainbridge Street yesterday morning, he discovered the body of an unknown white man floating in one of the docks . . . As there were no marks of violence on the body, it is thought that the man either committed suicide or fell overboard. He was about 45 years of age, five feet five inches tall, and weighed about 145 pounds. He had light reddish hair and a moustache of the same hue. His clothes consisted of a dark plaid sack coat, brown gaiters, a black striped shirt and brown overalls. The body was taken to the morgue, where at a late hour last night it still awaited identification.
>
> *Public Ledger*, October 19, 1900

The most likely place in which to locate officially overlooked suicides is in the drowning category. This is in fact considerably larger for 1868-1872 than for 1899-1901, and many individual cases must be regarded as doubtful. In drowning incidents juries applied one of two labels. "Accidentally drowned" was the term for those cases in which the element of accident could be firmly established, as by witnesses. The Scotch verdict "found drowned" in practice meant merely that the body had been discovered in the water. This subcategory in many years amounted to nearly half the total drownings and must have contained some suicides. Direct comparison of different periods is impossible, since these verdicts were recorded separately only for the years toward the end of the century, but if the proportion was close to constant over time, there were more "found drowned" in 1870 than in 1900. Drowning, at 6 percent of the recorded totals, was not officially a leading means of suicide, but it was still numerically important enough to warrant further examination.

Probably the cases in the drowning category, more than any other, do skew the difference between the real and the recorded incidence of suicide. The official figures, if the 6 percent for the later years may be read back for the earlier, would mean that only two or three people drowned themselves annually around 1870, and ten or twelve around 1900. But the newspapers in all periods indicate that *attempted* suicides by drowning were quite common. While the city offered no such traditional attractions as the Golden Gate or London bridges, its two great rivers, the Delaware and the Schuylkill, were apparently among the first places that occurred to persons in despair, and many must have found them successfully.

The fact that these people, once dead, did not all find their way into the same health-office totals does not indicate any consistent desire to conceal their motives, however; the "found drowned" verdict, which covered small boys and sailors as well as more obviously suicidal types, was as precise as most circumstances allowed. The absence of great spectacular bridges and similarly visible points of takeoff meant only that Philadelphians, with a perhaps characteristic lack of flair, simply slipped off banks and wharves unwitnessed. Most important for the argument here, there is no reason to suppose that adding these people to the suicide category would affect the relative, as distinct from the absolute, suicide rate, certainly not enough to affect the rise recorded for the last thirty years of the century. The greater number of drowning victims in the earlier period does create a larger pool in which to drag for unrecorded suicides. But again it is possible to set some outer limits to the number. It is most reasonable to suppose that some roughly constant proportion—10 percent, or 15 at the outside, of suicides were "found drowned." In the later years, when about 150 suicides were recorded annually, the number in the "found drowned" subcategory rarely reached 40; since most, according to newspaper reports, were obviously misfortunate fishermen and bathers, no more than 15 or 20 can reasonably be regarded as suspicious. For all who sought to resolve their problems in the water, far more trusted to the somewhat surer alternatives available in the home.

Few of these alternatives were ever officially listed as accidental. For the seventeen late-century years in which the breakdown of suicide means was listed, there were a total of 2,096 suicides reported; the leading means employed were, in order: shooting, 580 cases or 28 percent; poisoning, 488 or 23 percent; hanging, 448 or 21 percent; illuminating gas, 159 or 8 percent; and slashing, or stabbing, 151 or 7 percent.[10] In contrast to the remaining 13 percent, mostly drownings, casualties, and some more bizarre alternatives such as "setting hair on fire," very few cases in these leading categories could have been hidden elsewhere. Hanging was almost never listed as accidental, gunshot wounds only two or three times a year on the average, suffocation by gas two or three. Only cases of willful self-poisoning, if mislabeled, could have affected the suicide rate by more than a few percentage points, but that would increase rather than decrease the gap in the rates between the years around 1870 and those around 1900, since accidental poisoning was registered more commonly in the later years. An even 100 such incidents were reported for 1899-1901, as shown in Table 3. The aggregate rate of poisonings is considerably higher than in modern times, but the proportion of victims over fourteen years old, 82 percent, is not markedly higher, especially in comparison with the 139 suicidal poisonings recorded for the same three years; much or indeed all of the difference may be laid to the notorious range and nature of the nineteenth-century pharmacopoeia.[11]

The relative popularity of each of the listed suicide methods did vary with the availability of means, the state of popular medical knowledge, and perhaps fashion. The most important change was the growing use of handguns, especially from the 1840s through the 1860s, a phenomenon discussed more fully in chapter 4; by the 1880s at the latest, shooting was the most common means employed, followed by hanging, which seems always to have been second. During 1839-1841, before small revolvers came into general use, poison was the more usual route; only two men shot themselves to death in those three years, according to newspaper reports. Poison still held first place even in 1854-1857, three years for which full coroners' records are available. At the end of the century illuminating gas appeared on the record for the first time in 1889, with a single case; within a few years it had passed slashing to move into fourth place. The range of poisons available did expand as the century progressed, to a dozen or so by the end, but this did not occasion any dramatic increase in the proportion of suicides by overdose. Laudanum was always widely available as a cheap painkiller, and with arsenic and sometimes one or two others, provided an earlier generation with all it needed.

The rise in the overall suicide rate, then, cannot be explained either in terms of rising use of poisons or of rising accuracy in the diagnosis of this somewhat less violent or dramatic alternative. The conclusion remains that the only large number of suicides that may have escaped official report were those in which, then as now, a complaisant and sympathetic family doctor. long acquainted with the victim, quietly joined a conspiracy.

> The coroner was summoned yesterday morning, to hold an inquest on the body of a white woman, about 30 years of age, at the Moyamensing prison. Her name was Rachel Barrett, and she had been committed on Thursday evening as a vagrant, having been found in the street in a state of intoxication, without any home or shelter . . . The jury re-

turned a verdict that the deceased came to her death by
hanging herself.

Public Ledger, June 5, 1840

While his mind was temporarily deranged, the Reverend
Louis Rosenburg, a Lutheran clergyman, committed suicide by shooting. About two weeks ago he opened a small
mission at Fourth and Cypress Streets. He did not meet
with the success he desired, and became despondent . . .

Public Ledger, July 2, 1900

Once the long-term rise in the suicide rate has
been established as genuine, it is possible to investigate the reasons for it. And while there are no official figures devoted to the
question "why?" there are clues provided in those answering the
question "who?"

The serious study of self-destruction as a social phenomenon
began with the publication at the very end of the nineteenth
century of Emile Durkheim's classic book, *Suicide.* It was Durkheim's central contention that suicidal behavior was associated
in complex fashion with social status and that it was more common among the rich than the poor.[12] He also argued that it was
often precipitated by sudden changes in circumstance that were
great enough to leave the individual in a condition of "anomie,"
lost in a novel world without traditional rules or experience as
guides.[13] These two propositions are in fact linked; anomie is
more likely to beset mobile, sensitive, and highly placed persons than ordinary members of the working class. Both, along
with several of Durkheim's other suggestions, served as the conventional wisdom in sociological studies of suicide for decades
after their original formulation.

This conventional wisdom has been challenged more recently
at several points, and much of Durkheim's theory is not supported by the Philadelphia materials.[14] But the evidence, although some of it is complicated, does reinforce his original argument that suicide in the nineteenth century was committed
predominantly by people of relatively high status.

To the extent that status is a function of economic class, the
registration materials provide three sets of figures by which to

measure it. The one direct measure is incomplete and must be supplemented with evidence from outside Philadelphia. The other two measures are indirect. But when used all together, they make a coherent case.

The *Annual Register of Deaths* should provide the surest evidence about class, in that "occupation" is one of the items of information to be supplied on death certificates. In Philadelphia, however, this space was usually left blank. One of the few careful contemporary studies of nineteenth-century mortality includes Philadelphia for the six years between 1885 and 1890 and contains a table of deaths, including suicide, by occupation.[15] Dr. John S. Billings computed his totals from information apparently supplied by the health office; the number of suicides among male Philadelphians with listed occupations was 188 out of 13,159 deaths, indicating that 14 of every 1,000 deaths in the group was a suicide. He included, however, no column for "unclear" or "unknown" occupations. And his figures cover only a fraction, perhaps one-third, of all employable or adult males who died in the six-year period, a fraction that cannot safely be regarded as random. Thus, while his findings do generally indicate higher suicide rates among men who had more prestigious jobs, the numbers cannot be fully trusted.

Fortunately, however, Billings also supervised a much larger study of mortality for the Eleventh Census in 1890. Here, for certain areas in the northeast, the "registration states," instructions to participating physicians were fuller, and the figures for occupation are accordingly stronger. And although it appears that economic status was not the only or perhaps even the major determinant of male suicide rates (see chapter 6 and appendix C), the figures for these states do fill out the impression given by the sketchier ones for Philadelphia alone. Among all occupation groups of males over fifteen years old in the registration states, excluding those categories with less than 100,000 members, the most suicidal were "professional," with an age-standardized rate of 23.7 per 100,000, and "clerical and official," which included most businessmen, at 21.2. These were followed somewhat less predictably by "laboring and servant," at 17.6, "manufacturing and mechanical" at 17.0, "mercantile and trading"—largely peddlers and hucksters—at 12.7, with "agriculture, transport, and other outdoor" at 10.4.[16]

The other two possible measures of social class are less direct but more inclusive of the population of Philadelphia itself. They are residence by ward and nativity, either U.S. or foreign. The relative wealth of the city's wards can be established in several ways; it can safely be assumed also that the foreign-born were typically poorer than the natives. Neither measure, however, can be accepted at face value, since it cannot be shown that the suicides registered as living in a given ward or belonging to a given ethnic population were in any sense representative. It is an "ecological fallacy" to assume that all persons from rich neighborhoods were rich—some were servants or poor relations—or that foreign-born suicides were poorer than average because most immigrants were. But with this preliminary caveat, the two indices do prove useful.

The figures for the foreign-born are dramatic and at first reading seem to contradict both classical theory and the data from the studies by Dr. Billings. In 1870 there were about 184,000 immigrants living in Philadelphia, 27 percent of the population; their age-standardized rate of suicide during the five years 1868-1872 was 7.4 per 100,000, markedly higher than the 5.5 among natives.[17] In 1900 the foreign-born numbered about 295,000, down slightly to 23 percent of the whole; for 1899-1901 their suicide rate, adjusted to the same standard, had climbed to 14.6, compared to 11.8 among natives. In practice, especially during the years around 1870, the gap between the two populations was probably somewhat larger than these figures indicate; in any case, all such calculations suggest provisionally that poverty, through foreignness, was associated with suicide.[18]

The figures for residence, although ultimately more convincing, are less striking at first. Of the several possible measures of the relative prosperity of Philadelphia's political wards, perhaps the best, and certainly for present purposes the most appropriate, is the death rate. This rate indicates relative density, standards of cleanliness, availability of medical attention, and family size, nineteenth-century death rates being highest among the very young. The rate varied quite substantially; in one ward one resident in twenty-nine died each year, in another one in seventy. Several wards scored in the thirties and the sixties in both periods. The bearing of this rate upon suicide may be measured in two ways. One procedure is to divide the city in half, comparing the healthiest twenty of the forty-one wards of 1900 with the unhealthiest and similarly splitting the twenty-seven wards of 1870 into two groups of thirteen. The other method is to compare the extremes, the five best and worst wards of 1900, the six best and worst of 1870 (the latter procedure necessitated by a tie).[19] In both methods, the next step is to add up several years of suicides by ward and to compare the rates.

The results are surprising. For the earlier period, five years of suicides show an average rate, for the wards in both top and bottom halves, of just 5.4 per 100,000, with the thirteen unhealthiest wards a shade less suicidal. For the three years around 1900, the rate was 10.2 for the healthiest half, 11.2 for the unhealthiest. At the extremes, the rate for the worst six wards in the earlier period was 8.7; for the best six, 10.0. This is reversed, by an equally insignificant margin, for the period around 1900, with the best five wards scoring 11.8, and the worst, 13.0. In short, the residential index appears to show no appreciable economic class difference among the suicides of either period.

But neither the nativity nor the residential indices proves what it appears to prove on first reading. The residential index has one clear flaw, which is that the older Delaware River wards, the poorest, were credited with a number of suicide cases that did not really belong there. Each year a number of unidentified persons were counted in the figures (see chapter 4). Already in 1870 and decidedly by 1900, much of the downtown had been abandoned as a residential area by the richer citizens. Not only the anonymous drowners but also the unidentified transients who took gas in lonely hotel rooms artificially swelled the total for these poorer districts.

Except for that, the use of residence as an index of the economic position of suicides is actually not so inconclusive as it might seem. It is hard to imagine circumstances in which the "ecological fallacy" could invalidate the results obtained, given the remarkably even distribution of suicide through the wards.

If indeed it was the coachmen and laundresses who were being counted for the wealthy thirty-second ward, they must have been balanced by equally unrepresentative types, hoteliers, perhaps, or ship captains, from the first. The results are the same in the end.

And when these results are considered not in isolation, but together with those for the nativity index, the picture clearly changes. The foreign-born, with high suicide rates, tended to live in the poorer wards, thus raising the rate for those wards and depressing the rate for the richer. If it were possible to hold this factor constant, to somehow subtract the immigrants from the population—the Irish and Germans of 1870, joined by the Jews, Slavs, and Italians of 1900—the result would show that economic class *did* make a difference. Among the remainder, the native-born, the rate of suicide would be revealed as considerably higher in the rich than in the poor sections of Philadelphia.

> Twelve Germans, recently from Germany by way of New York, ten males and two females, were brought up by the watchman . . . (who) found one of the men weltering in his blood but alive . . . The doctor visited the place in the morning, and discovered at the head of the stairway a rope and suspenders with blood on them, attached to an upright post; this induced the belief that the man had attempted in a double way to take his own life . . . The two women were examined, who, through an interpreter, testified that the first they knew of the circumstances was his crying out to them to get some one to pray for him, that he had cut his throat and would die . . .
>
> *Public Ledger*, August 6, 1840

The finding about class and suicide among native citizens suggests the need for a second look at the meaning of the suicide rate among immigrants. For most purposes, the "foreignness" of a given population may be a reasonable measure of its poverty, but perhaps not with respect to suicide. If it is difficult to imagine ways, as explained above, in which the possibly unrepresentative character of the suicides in each ward could invalidate the use of the residential index, it is easy to imagine that the foreign suicides were not evenly distributed throughout the spectrum of immigrants. In general some ethnic groups had very high rates, and others had low ones; the sharp differences recorded in the nineteenth century, the result of contrasting cultural traditions, were more easily measured in this country than in the homeland since here all groups were subject to the same suicide registration process. The study by Dr. Billings shows that among the principal groups that immigrated to Philadelphia throughout the period, those born in Germany tended to be several times more suicidal than those born in Ireland; the rates for the latter almost certainly would have registered lower than those for native Americans if it were possible to adjust for differences in the age structures of the two populations.[20] For the wider registration area in the 1890 census, the crude suicide rates, as distinguished by the mother's birthplace, were: United States, 5.0 per 100,000; Ireland, 5.3; Germany, 16.0. The Italians were also relatively low, at 6.4; the Bohemians were listed at 22.1; the Hungarians, 28.0.[21] Thus in the context of suicide, what the U.S.-foreign distinction may measure is difference not in class but in culture; Bohemians of either high or low estate were measurably more self-destructive than most natives of whatever economic condition.

Durkheim's famous theory about anomie is difficult to assess, finally, but to the degree that it is accepted, it suggests that the association between suicide and immigration may be explicable in terms of something less tangible than the poverty of newcomers to the United States. Anomie is a condition that would surely often arise, if anywhere, from those bewildering changes in personal situation that beset transplanted aliens. Those changes were not directly material, as measured by the transition from poverty in the Old World to poverty in the New, but rather psychic, of a kind that might afflict the comfortable, the dancing master as easily as the hod carrier.

If this is the case, as it appears, the evidence then fits. While not separately conclusive, all of it weighed together makes sense both theoretically and empirically. And it indicates that while suicide rates in nineteenth-century Philadelphia were determined by many factors, they were generally higher among the upper than the lower classes, almost certainly for natives and quite probably for immigrants as well.

> Yesterday Mr. John Halberstadt, well known in our community as an active, busy, member of society, and formerly an extensive merchant, was found dead in bed, at the Mansion House, South Third Street, having, as it subsequently appeared, died some time during the night from the effects of drinking morphine. Mr. H. was generally known by the cognomen of "Baron Halberstadt," and was about 42 years of age . . . it is thought that reverses of fortune, in conjunction with a distressing malady, may have induced the awful deed.
>
> *Public Ledger,* December 30, 1840

There are dimensions other than economic for calculating personal status, and along these the conclusions are clearer than are those for class. Historically in Philadelphia as in American society generally, suicide has been committed disproportionately by adult white males, although other groups have been moving closer. And that white male pattern, strong for the twentieth century, was far stronger for the late nineteenth.

Table 4 partially illustrates the situation for three periods. The rates shown in the table for the years 1969-1971 should illuminate some of the differences in the patterns for the previous century. The very high incidence for white males, especially toward the end of the century, resulted largely from two conditions: the higher proportion of suicidal immigrant groups, as compared to more recent times, and the higher proportion of men in suicidal occupations of the sort that have left the city in the later twentieth century. But high rates for adult white men did not result in markedly higher rates for the nineteenth-century population as a whole, as the table shows, because they were balanced by very low rates for women, for minors, and for blacks.[22]

There are no rates for blacks in Table 4 because the numbers for the first two periods are so low that they simply do not warrant calculation. But the pattern for blacks, if shown, would be an extreme version of the one evident for women: a continuous rise in the suicide rate from 1870 to the end of the century and indeed into the present. But it is a rise that begins from a very small base, in this case insignificantly small. Philadelphia's

Table 4. Average annual age-standardized suicide rates per 100,000
for selected groups, 1868-1872, 1899-1901, 1969-1971.[1]

Group	1868-1872	1899-1901	1969-1971
All persons	5.8	12.2	11.4
All whites	6.0	12.6	12.4
White males	11.0	19.5	13.3
White females	2.0	5.2	10.8

Source: See appendix A.
1. The standard population used is that for Philadelphia in 1900.

black population in 1870 was a little over 22,000 persons, 3.3
percent of the whole; in 1900 it was about 62,000, or 4.9 percent. Over this entire period, only 21 suicides were recorded for
the entire group, 14 of them after 1889.

No separate figures for minors are given in the table; if they
were they would fit the same pattern. As with blacks, the numbers, especially for the period around 1870, are not large
enough to be included in Table 4. Between 1860 and 1901, of
over 3,000 suicides reported, only 87 involved minors. As with
women and blacks, the number was moving up toward the end
of the period—over half were recorded after 1889—but it was
still only a fraction of the modern rate.

> Ida Claus, aged 16 of Stanley Street, below Huntingdon,
> died yesterday at the Women's Homeopathic Hospital of
> the effects of drinking Carbolic Acid with suicidal intent,
> on Wednesday night, at the home of a friend . . . Ida was
> an orphan, and resided at the Stanley Street address with
> Mrs. Sarah Fluck, her sister . . . There was a note . . . In it
> she asked her friend to forgive her for what she had done.
> She said that she wanted to die because a young man she
> had been intimate with had ceased to care for her . . .
> *Public Ledger*, December 14, 1900

Suicide is to some degree a construct of the social imagination; a society finds it where it searches and may
not recognize it in unexpected places. But the low suicide rates
of the three low-status groups—minors, blacks, and women—
cannot be explained in terms of social or official blind spots.

The Philadelphia *Public Ledger* throughout the period treated suicide as news and often as an opportunity for the brief expression of moral opinion or sentiment. The press was influential, certainly, among suicides themselves; it appears that in the nineteenth-century city, as now, individuals were often inspired to act by examples provided in the news.[23] The *Ledger* and its contemporaries generally shared none of our modern delicacy; "Suicide" and "Apparent Suicide" were frequent headlines, sometimes anticipating as well as following official verdicts. And the brief accounts, most of them cumulatively monotonous in their sameness, always attempted at the end to explain the business in something less than a dozen words.

Inquest juries took the matter of explanation with some seriousness, and witnesses were brought in to testify to the state of the decedent's mind as well as body. Mystery sometimes remained, in cases of allegedly healthy and prosperous men with families, or promising youths, or cheerful serving girls. But usually the events seemed to point toward one of seven causes or categories, into which virtually all cases could be squeezed. Genuine insanity was rather rare, but financial troubles or reverses, domestic problems, romantic frustration, dissolution, disgrace, and incurable illness seemed to encompass everything that witnesses, jurors, and reporters could imagine.

Three of these categories, not counting the mysterious, were certainly applicable to minors: the romantic most especially and sometimes the dissolute and disgraceful. Although in life the three categories might sometimes be entangled, and older folk were allowed to have illicit involvements, the *Ledger* carefully tried to keep them separate, especially among the young. There was in 1841 a revealing incident in which, under the headline "Love and Suicide," the paper sounded more than usually excited over the discovery in the Schuylkill River of the bodies of two young people, tied together at the wrists and furnished further with pistols in their pockets, evidently for use should courage fail at water's edge.[24] Next day the editor felt the need to apologize to his readers, as the bodies had been found to belong to persons of ill repute, a quondam servant girl who had recently been "kept" by an unknown party and the heir of a respectable Chester County family, who was gambling his way down through Philadelphia's lowest quarter. Since such persons were clearly incapable of any truly exalted emotion, the explanation had to be changed; it was supposed that shame, wretchedness, and impending poverty must have led them to the deed. The editor's disappointment was evident. Dissolution was always newsworthy, an occasion for the implicit and explicit moralizing that was such an important function of the nineteenth-century press, but nothing beat romance. A young suicide, especially a young woman, was always fraught with possibilities for both sentimental and prurient imaginations. And until a positive identification, which was not always made, any female not outrageously unqualified might pass in death for under twenty-one.

The problem of black suicide, or its absence, is different but parallel to that of minors. The usual explanations—except perhaps disgrace, which implied the possession of honor to begin with, and the subcategory of financial reverses—were not in any obvious way incompatible with contemporary views of Negro character. The *Ledger*, in the same month in which it was unwilling to admit the possibility of serious passion among the immoral, was willing to ascribe a black girl's overdose to the discovery that her beloved was already married.[25] None could deny that terminal illness and family problems beset blacks at least as often as whites. Nor did white officialdom systematically ignore the black community, as it did in traditionally segregated areas. On the contrary the coroner in particular spent a disproportionate amount of time in black neighborhoods, simply because so many residents died without medical attention and so required a viewing and a certificate before burial, often in "City Ground."

The underrepresentation of women, finally, cannot be interpreted in terms other than the obvious. Except, like blacks, for explanations involving responsibility for financial reverses, they too were subject to all of the ills thought to lead through despondency to death. The contemporary understanding of suicide had room for them as well as for the other important groups that were underrepresented in the registration figures; if they were not often listed, it appears simply that they were not often there.

> Dear Sir:
>   I wish it to be distinctly understood, that I am not laboring under any insanity, hallucination, or aberration of mind, but am in my senses, true reason, and judgement. If I am not now sane I never was sane in my life—and consequently if you report me as above for the sake of our clergy, you will tell a deliberate lie.
>   It is a satiety of existence, disgust for the world, a longing for repose, and contempt for men. I never asked to come here—I was thrust here, and most unquestionably have a right to go to sleep when I like. I am yours etc.,
>   John H. Lehr
>   Note addressed to the coroner, reprinted
>   in the *Public Ledger*, August 25, 1841

Those white male adults who did populate the suicide totals were not typically scorned by their contemporaries for taking their own lives. Philadelphia was heir to an Anglo-American culture that had never regarded suicide with the horror demanded by Catholic tradition. There is little evidence of official cheating in large part because there was relatively little social pressure for it. There was a formula for dealing with at least some of those cases in which the feelings of the family were apparently at issue: "Suicide by _____ , committed in a fit of temporary insanity." (Indeed the insanity "defense," it has been claimed, together with the relatively honest statistical reportage which it enabled, contributed heavily to Britain's reputation among its continental neighbors as a land of gloomy madmen.)[26]

The press treated the issue as directly as it did because it apparently neither encountered nor encouraged much reticence. The official view, with its insistence upon sin and crime, was rarely challenged directly, but it was honored mostly in the breach and undercut in a variety of ways. The conservative *Ledger* could treat self-destruction as a fit subject for joking, as in an "Address to Throat Cutters," a bit of doggerel whose second verse advises:

When well resolved, from fortune rough
You sit with Razors, grinning
Pray let your neck be bare enough
Lest Ye should spoil your linen.[27]

The paper could even suggest, during the craze for the new science of phrenology, that suicide might well be determined, the product of some physical cause. Underdevelopment of the cranial organs governing hope, caution, and "vivativeness" clearly required sympathetic treatment rather than sermonizing.[28]

Except in the case of the dissolute, the truly insane, or the irresponsible—those who left their families to charity—the *Ledger* never expressed condemnation. The view that the act was in any way cowardly found no support, perhaps because it was most often performed by those substantial white male citizens who were thought most courageous. The death of John Lehr, whose note is reproduced above, was treated, in typical fashion, with a mixture of wonder tinged with admiration. The overused adjective "awful" was fully appropriate for the self-destruction of a successful man in his middle thirties, one of those in the inexplicable category, an artist who left careful instructions for the completion of his father's portrait. For a few others caught in untenable situations, lawsuits or failed examinations or unpayable loans, suicide seemed a gentlemanly if mistaken thing to do. For the chronically ill, there was the same note of sympathy that a modern middle-class observer might sound.

> No cause can as yet be ascribed for the rash and melancholy deed.
> Formula for the end of suicide accounts
> in the *Public Ledger*

The surviving materials do not permit any easy speculation as to what suicide meant personally to those who chose it, or even what conjunction of social and emotional circumstances led some groups to commit it in patterns different from those prevailing now. Many reasons were so unique and private as to defy social analysis of any sort. Although many

other explanations taken collectively do indicate important social trends, fuller discussion must follow an investigation of
other sorts of violent death, to which suicide seems in varying
ways related.

But a few preliminary observations may be made, or repeat-
ed. The rate of suicide was rising, sharply so after 1870. Also it
was rising in "progressive" fashion—if progress is defined simply as movement toward the future, in which less privileged
groups, such as women, children, and blacks, were counted
more often. And suicide seems in a double sense to be an index
of "civilization": it was associated both with the growth of the
city and with those sorts of people who were or had been most
involved in its economic organization and culture.

CHAPTER 3

ACCIDENT

> Man has a persistent tendency to tamper with his environ-
> ment and so lives in one of his own making, frequently
> without anticipating the consequences.
>
> Albert P. Iskrant and Paul V. Joliet,
> *Accidents and Homicide*

Simple accident is a subject of less intrinsic human interest than either homicide or suicide. Almost nothing
relevant has been written about its history or sociology, and the
sources are nearly as brief as the bibliography. With a few spectacular exceptions, a line or two in a coroner's report or newspaper is all that records any given accident in nineteenth-century Philadelphia. But if only because of the greater numbers
involved and the relatively noncontroversial nature of their collection and registration, the changing indices of accident are in
some ways more important than suicide or homicide in providing a rough quantitative dimension to the study of behavioral
change during Philadelphia's industrial age.

For the three most important kinds of accident, the figures are
at first sight meaningless or even contradictory.[1] As with suicide in chapter 2, the sixty-three years from 1839 to 1901 are divided into nine seven-year intervals, to show the incidence of
fatality per 100,000, as in Table 5.

Table 5.   Crude average annual accident rates per 100,000 population, by period, 1839-1901.

Years	Casualties	Burns and scalds	Drownings
1839-1845	10.5	7.4	16.5
1846-1853	14.2	8.8	16.6
1854-1859	25.6	9.1	19.8
1860-1866	23.2	11.4	19.5
1867-1873	28.6	10.7	18.0
1874-1880	24.4	8.9	15.0
1881-1887	34.8	8.2	10.6
1888-1894	41.7	8.3	8.8
1895-1901	39.5	11.3	7.8

Source: See appendix A.

The problems these numbers present are different from those in chapter 2. With suicide, the major difficulty is verification of the figures; apart from motive, there is no question as to physical responsibility for death, which rests by definition with the victim. But accident typically results from the conjunction of two kinds of agency, human and technological. A fall from a precipice on a still day is a different matter from an unexpected boiler explosion. What Table 5 records, at least in the first two categories, is changing combinations of elements. To interpret it, it is necessary to determine how much results from the behavior of people on the scene and how much results from technology, especially the new industrial technology of the later nineteenth century. It is this last factor that creates the apparent contradictions; once it has been accounted for, the reality behind the figures turns out to be much simpler than the table indicates at first sight.

> The body of a man who was killed by a train near the Germantown and Norristown Railroad Bridge, near 20th Street, last Friday night, has been identified as that of John Hermanson, 32 years, of 1729 Juniata Street. He was employed at the Midvale Steel Works, and was on his way home when he was killed.
>
> Public Ledger, January 14, 1901

The most complicated of the three major types of accident is "casualties" and the minor categories associated with it. The word itself almost never appears on death certificates; the category is an artificial one, created by the health office to cover a variety of lethal mishaps. The common denominator is not the medical but the circumstantial cause of death, not "skull fracture" but "train wreck."

Some types of accident, especially falls by people not at work, are as old as the species. Trees overhead proved fatally attractive to young men, as ice underfoot was fatally treacherous to old women; one Philadelphian was gored to death by an elk in 1892, another by an elephant in 1886. Other sorts of mishaps dated from the invention of roofs, wheels, and stairways.

But most casualties were related to making a living in the money economy. If the victim was not at work, it often happened that he was struck down by men who were. Failing eyes and reflexes kept the numbers of accidents to the elderly high. Both in 1869-1871 and 1899-1901, the highest casualty *rates* recorded were for people in their sixties and older, although because of their relatively small numbers their *totals* were not very great. Children and teenagers, on the other hand, had nearly as many accidents as people in their twenties, the result of dodging in and out of traffic, scaling fences, and teasing horses; however, because of their larger numbers in the population, their rates were not so high. Females of all ages were victimized less than one-fifth as often as males, a disproportion that was almost certainly greater among those in the prime of life.

Many working accidents, too, might have occurred as easily in the time of William Penn or Ramses II, the result of falls from masts and scaffolds, collapsing walls, collisions with loaded wagons and fractious animals. These account for the majority of the casualties of 1840 and many of those of 1900. But the long and sometimes sharp rise in accidents recorded in Table 5 was obviously the result of newer ways of making a living, principally in manufactories and on railroads. The figures reflect the sorts of people who held the more dangerous jobs, which were generally tough but by no means the least desirable. According to Dr. Billings's study of deaths from 1885 to 1890, transportation, construction, farm labor, and factory work led the list of hazardous jobs.[2] The black population, generally barred from such work, was slightly underrepresented among victims, the foreign-born more heavily overrepresented.

Aside from the somewhat limited data on occupations, it is impossible to find out just what proportions of these deaths were attributable to which industries. But the coroners did grant separate listing to one major source of accidents, in later years by far the leading violent killer in Philadelphia: the railroad. The period covered, in fact, encompasses the development of railroading from its infancy to its apogee. In 1839 the first track in the United States was only a decade old, and from Philadelphia one could ride no farther west than Harrisburg. In 1901 the directors of the giant Pennsylvania Railroad, still unable to hear the hum of automobile engines, issued $600,000,000 worth of capital stock.[3] Meanwhile the number of fatal casualties in the city served almost as a barometer of this growth.

The death rate from railroads was a matter of concern on several levels. There were no workmen's compensation laws in that period, and few carried commercial life insurance. Major employers customarily paid funeral expenses in cases of fatal injury, but according to the one relevant study, of Pittsburgh in 1906-07, fewer than half of the victims' families received any other compensation.[4] The Pennsylvania Railroad, beginning in 1886, sponsored a widely copied benefit association, at minimal cost to itself, as a device for avoiding liability; but with workmen as with others, if anything else was at stake, the matter was left to the rivalry between contingency lawyers and claims agents.[5]

Here the judgment of a coroner's jury could be critically important. In most cases an inquest verdict consisted simply of pronouncing a probable cause of death after hearing the relevant medical and other testimony. In a few cases the verdict suggested human responsibility, as in homicide and suicide, occasionally medical malpractice or negligence. Since juries rarely censured anyone, especially the victims, the absence of any assignment of blame was not, presumably, decisive in case of lawsuit. But a deliberate censure could be, precisely because it occurred so seldom. The political atmosphere of nineteenth-century Philadelphia cannot be considered hostile to corporations in general and railroads in particular, and the coroners as a class were perhaps as well inclined toward the great roads as toward the petty lawyers who represented the victims. But when the juries did return censure verdicts, the railroad companies were usually the targets. In 1854-1857, there were just eight censures, against three doctors, one druggist, one contractor, one landlord, one canal boat captain—and the North Penn Railroad, for an accident on July 17, 1857, which killed twenty-one persons, eleven of them Philadelphians.[6] In 1878-1880, the only other period for which full dockets exist, there were twenty-seven censures—twenty-one of them directed at the railroads, for such faults as excessive speed, failure to provide proper signals, and poorly lit conditions.[7]

Late in the century these protestations and others, from newspaper campaigns to official condemnation by the secretary of state of internal affairs, may have had some effect on street railways.[8] The greatest proportion of fatalities on these intraurban routes occurred immediately after electrification in the early 1890s; horses had an instinct for avoiding pedestrians that moving machines did not. Within a few years some simple safety precautions somewhat reduced the number of these deaths. But the great steam roads rolled on and over unheeding. During the first generation of their operation, big wrecks such as the North Penn disaster were not uncommon. These were greatly reduced in later years, and as the companies insisted, the passengers were safe enough—once they had managed to get aboard. But primitive safety standards continued to take a heavy toll of employees; almost incredibly, accidents accounted for well over half of all deaths among the city's blue-collar railroad workers from 1885 to 1890.[10] And deaths of employees amounted to only one-quarter to one-third of all railway deaths registered; pedestrians, especially the young and the old, paid the heaviest price.[11] The number of fatalities of all sorts climbed almost as a function of traffic mileage. The first year for which any coroner's figures are available is 1855, the last 1900. All available totals, including those from horse railways, are listed in Table 6.

Although these scattered figures cannot be extrapolated with any confidence, it is possible with the help of other information to calculate that around 1870 about thirty people were killed in railroad accidents annually.[12] Thirty years later this largest single component of the casualties category had multiplied by a factor of five and accounted for roughly as many fatal accidents, in proportion to population, as motor vehicles in the modern city.[13]

The railroad was simply the most dramatic symbol of the Age of Industry. Already by 1840 and clearly by 1870, technological progress had created several new sets of dangerous possibilities. By 1900, in addition to the increased use and higher speed of whirring machinery and the greater height of buildings using structural steel, man's inventiveness had created even more means of dying. Stock clerks slipped down elevator shafts, old men fell into open manholes, young ones ran bicycles into immovable objects, citizens of all ages tangled with live electric wires.

For the last thirty years of the century it is possible to calculate very roughly the changes in the accident rate, with results that reveal something about changing behavior. The aim is to estimate how much of the difference resulted from a changing level of careless or reckless individual action, as distinct from

Table 6.   Number of street and steam railway casualties, by year.

Year	No. killed	Year	No. killed	Year	No. killed
1855	20	1884	139	1893	216
1856	19	1885	121	1894	236
1874	55	1886	153	1895	221
1875	40	1888	166	1896	199
1878	72	1889	143	1897	145
1879	84	1890	193	1899	167
1880	105	1891	176	1900	168
1882	128	1892	208		

Source: See appendix A.

that which resulted from changes in the technological or physical environment.

The first step is to define more accurately the real rate of accidental death. Casualties, as an artificial category, covered most, but not all accidents other than burns, scalds, and drownings. Distinct records were kept of certain others, which must be added in. They include "strangulation," "gunshot wounds," and "tetanus," which contemporary physicians understood as associated with puncture wounds and invariably fatal within a day or two.[14] "Asphyxia" and "suffocation" seem to have been interchangeable, although there was a tendency over time to use the former term for infant deaths and the latter for persons dying of inhalation of smoke or gas. (In the counts that follow, deaths of infants from either of these causes are omitted because they may have been cases of "crib death.") A few incidents, moreover, that might have been lumped under casualties were for unexplained and inexplicable reasons listed under separate headings. Among these are "fractures," listed by type; "shock," which was understood, then as now, to result from traumatic injury; and "compression of the brain" and "concussion of the brain," which were interchangeable with each other and sometimes with "skull fracture" as well. "Electric shock" is clear enough. But even counting all of these additional categories, the list is still conservative. It excludes most problematic cases and includes, in effect, only those who died instantly or within a very few days. While the last thirty years of the century did not witness any significant advance in the treatment of shock or maiming, there were improvements in dealing with infection, "septicemia," and "gangrene." Thus these categories, "surgical shock," and ambiguous categories such as "hemorrhage" are not included—nor are "Bright's disease," "erysipelas," and a few others which, by the evidence of coroner's returns, include some victims of sudden violence.

All together these "minor" categories add up to about a third of the number of casualties for 1869-1871, somewhat less for 1899-1901. When they are added in, the fatal accident rate for the two periods seems very similar. It follows that, since technology accounted for more fatalities around 1900, simple human error, as in "falls," must have been proportionately more common around 1870. And it is possible to estimate that proportion by attempting, somewhat crudely, to discount the impact of technological advance, in order to calculate what the rate for the 1900 population might have been under the physical conditions of 1870.

This calculation requires four steps, beginning with the number of casualties and allied deaths in 1870—314—and in 1900—618. The first step is to standardize for the differing age structures in the two census years, a process that makes a greater difference in this case than in most others; it can be estimated that because of the greater proportion of older persons in 1900, the number of accidental deaths in 1870, given the same distribution of ages, would have been 340 rather than 314. The next step, numerically the most important, is to eliminate differences caused wholly by the expansion of the railways. The railroad deaths for 1870 can be estimated at 33; extrapolated to the size of the 1900 population, this would be 63. The actual number of railroad deaths in 1900 was 168, 105 more than the extrapolated figure. Subtracting 105 from the original 1900 death total of 618 leaves 513. The next two steps depend upon newspaper reports of deaths, which are undercounted and somewhat hard to compare.[15] The 1870 deaths directly attributable to machinery—persons dying instantly from being caught in belting or shafting or the like—were reported at 17, which extrapolates to 33 in 1900; the actual newspaper total for such incidents in the latter year was 53, an excess of 20. In addition, step three, in 1900 there were 19 new types of death reported, as from electric shock. These two net differences, 20 and 19, subtracted from the previous total of 513, leave 474. With a rounded population of 1,294,000 in 1900, 474 deaths amounts to a fatal accident rate of 36.6 per 100,000; for 1870, calculated from 340 deaths in a rounded population of 674,000, the rate would be 50.0 per 100,000. The drop in the rate, then, would be something more than 25 percent—a figure that would almost certainly be greater if a way could be found to discount more accurately all of the differences in the working environment.

Of course, the use of any specific number for such a difference implies a false precision, and the procedure sketched above may be flawed as well as crude. But the tendency indicated can be found elsewhere and by other means, as shown below.

> Deputy Coroner John C. Sees held an inquest yesterday in the case of Annie Groetzinger, aged 14 years, who died at St. Mary's hospital on Sunday Evening last from burns received by her clothing taking fire from coal oil that she poured upon a slow fire to hasten its burning. At the time she was employed as a domestic in the family of Mr. Henry Goebel, 1123 Mascher St.
>
> *Public Ledger,* December 1, 1870

The results reached in the case of casualties seem confirmed by an analysis of burns and scalds, the other major category of dry land accident.

It is virtually impossible to compare the type and incidence of fires in Philadelphia in 1839 and in 1901, or even for any significant stretch of years in between. Alexander Blackburn, America's first fire marshal, was appointed in Philadelphia in 1856 and held office for fifteen years. His reports and those of his successors supplement the ones issued by the fire department itself, providing an embarrassment of undigested statistical information about the nature, number, and causes of all fires.[16] Read literally, the figures indicate that firemen were called to deal with more incidents over time, but each incident did much less damage. In 1869-1871, the number of fire calls reported was about 587 annually, at a total cost of $2,660,000; in 1899-1901 the number averaged 2,940, and cost $3,387,000. But because of the number of variables involved, such as insurance coverage and practices, fluctuations in the price level, the sobriety of firemen and the number of call boxes, the literal comparison is misleading.

For fatal accidents, however, such comparison is unnecessary. Firemen and others trapped in burning buildings died then as now of suffocation. But these big fires did not contribute much to the burns and scalds category. Newspapers and coroners rarely reported more than one such fatality from the same incident or address; the exceptions were usually involved in scalds from boiler explosions. By attempting to answer the question, "who was killed?" rather than simply, "how many?" it is possible to deduce something about change over time.

During the period 1869-1871, the age-standardized rate of death from burns and scalds was 9.3; by 1900 it had advanced to 11.4. But this statistic is ultimately less revealing than the set that results from breaking the totals into age groups, as shown in Table 7.

The long generation at the end of the century witnessed a great increase in the industrial use of fire, fuels, and explosive chemicals, as well as the introduction of electric power. (Perhaps it was electricity, in combination with other new agents and operations, that accounted for the rise in the death rate from burns during the later 1880s and 1890s, after the dip beginning in the 1870s.) One result of this progress is reflected in the somewhat higher proportion of working people, adults, who died of burns and scalds toward century's end. But only a minority, at any time, died from incidents at work in the money economy outside of the home. Throughout the entire period the majority were victims of household incidents, especially in kitchens.

The collective profile of persons who died from burns and scalds is strikingly different from that of other victims of sudden violence. Most accidents, other than those falls to which old people were especially subject, involved males in the active years between the early teens and the middle fifties, either as agents or principals. But the domestic nature of most burnings and scaldings is shown by the fact that in the reports that make the distinction, in many years women outnumbered men, and minors almost always outnumbered adults. The general tendency for girls to outnumber boys suggests that such accidents often occurred as part of the socialization process, to children helping out, learning the woman's role. Among those under five —toddlers who tipped over boiling laundry tubs or swatted flies around lighted lamps—there was presumably less difference between the sexes.

Death in these cases often resulted from such classic homely ingredients as flaming grease or boiling water. But increasingly

Table 7. Deaths from burns and scalds: 3-year totals and average annual age-specific rates for adults and small children, 1869-1871 and 1899-1901.

Years	Adults 20 and over		Children 4 and under	
	Number	Rate	Number	Rate
1869-1871	82	7.0	99	42.9
1899-1901	180	7.8	150	38.1

Source: See appendix A.

in the late nineteenth century it was caused by newer and more volatile fluids. It is difficult to learn anything statistically about the ordinary domestic technology of heating, lighting, and cooking in this period. About 1840 the simplest wood or charcoal stoves, and candles, were still common. The accident table itself is probably the best gauge of the continued substitution of liquid fuels for solid over the next two or three decades. The earliest reported as cause of fatality was camphene, a mixture of turpentine and alcohol used in lamps. By the 1860s this primitive stuff had been replaced entirely by coal oil or petroleum distillates, benzine, naphtha, and kerosene, often in mixtures, and other similar products. By that time, the peak on the graph, most households had passed beyond wood and candle culture, to the great distress of the excitable Marshal Blackburn. These fluids were all dangerous. To break or spill an oil lamp, especially while wearing the heavy and awkward clothing that burdened the women of the period, was to risk severe burns; indeed, a lighted lamp was sometimes used as a murder weapon. Even more dangerous was the explosive flashback that could result when fuel was poured from an enclosed can onto an open flame.

At the end of the period the situation was again changing. Some kitchens and homes were using more modern appliances; illuminating gas and gasoline stoves had come to many, coal-burning central furnaces to some, electricity to a few. The problem posed is, what did these changes mean in terms of relative safety?

The kitchens and households of 1840 were obviously less dangerous than those of either 1870 or 1900. And the difference between 1870 and 1900, if not as sharp, is almost equally clear, although the official estimates are not as useful on this point as they might be. Blackburn's, in particular, are a charming blend of vagueness and misplaced precision; his first report, for 1856, lists "Accident, 89," as the most important cause of fire, followed by a long list of such particulars as "Boys Smoking Cigars in Lofts While Hunting Pigeons, 2." The more impersonal tallies of later years are considerably duller and only slightly more illuminating.[17] But one item does stand out. From 1870 until the end of the century, oil lamps were reported as the most frequent source of accidental fires. But by then a new hazard, unknown in 1870, held very close in second place. Domestic historians agree that gasoline stoves became widely popular sometime in the 1880s; perhaps even more than the newly introduced electricity, they account for the upsurge in burning deaths noted in Table 7.[18] Whatever their importance for housewifery, or perhaps cuisine, the most dramatic effect of these devices was to fill "the newspapers of that era with items about death and destruction incident to explosions in kitchens in which they had been installed."[19]

These dangers do not seem to have been concentrated in any narrow class or neighborhood. It is impossible to estimate how many people were trading wood stoves for gasoline, while others were substituting gas or electric lighting for kerosene, and others moved up from candles to lamps. But it appears that by 1900 the hazards had evened out and spread almost equally across the spectrum of class. It is not significant for my purposes that blacks and the foreign-born were slightly overrepresented among victims; blacks and immigrants were overrepresented in kitchens generally, because they managed not only their own but other people's, as servant girls and cooks. But if the object is to find differences in the physical character of households, quite apart from who lit the fires, then the index used in chapter 2 of rich and poor wards is an appropriate measure, and it shows that there was little difference in the number of burn fatalities.[20] Among the twenty poorest wards in 1899-1901, the three-year average death rate from burns and scalds was 12.0; among the twenty richest it was 11.0. At the extremes, the poorest five had a rate of 13.7; the richest five, 11.2. The slightly worse record for the poorer wards may reflect not a difference in domestic danger but rather the substantial minority of such accidents that occurred among blue-collar workers outside of the home and the deaths of servants who did not live in but were counted from the homes of their natural families.

By any measure, then, Philadelphians all over the city, in and out of the home, found their environment more hazardous around 1900 than it had been earlier, yet the death rate in the home was not rising but actually falling slightly, as indicated by the figures for the very young in Table 7. There is no physical fact that accounts for this drop—indeed, all physical changes would suggest the opposite effect. The explanation appears to lie not in the material environment of households and kitchens but in the behavior of the people who lived in them. The care of children is the responsibility of adults, and the parents and older siblings of 1870 seem typically to have been more careless than those of 1900, more likely to leave little ones untended or untaught, less habituated to routine precautions but perhaps more to mixing drinking alcohol with other liquid fuels.

> Fred Spowhouse and Alfred Edwards, aged 22 years, residing respectively at 1064 German Road and 1214 Palethorpe Street, were drowned, yesterday, in the Delaware, near Beiderman's Point, back of Petty's Island . . . No attention was paid to them until they were seen struggling in the water, when, before they could be aided, they were drowned. When the bodies were recovered, about 2 P.M., Edwards had Spowhouse in his arms, and it was supposed that they were drowned while the former was trying to rescue his friend . . .
>
> *Public Ledger,* August 13, 1870

The last major accident category is also by far the simplest. Drowning, in the great majority of cases, was accident pure and simple, without any significant technological component, the result of the elementary human miscalculation of risk. And no other index shows a more dramatic drop over time, as can be seen from Table 5, especially during the critical period beginning about 1870. During 1869-1871 the age-standardized drowning rate was 18.5 per 100,000.[21] By 1899-1901 it had dropped to 8.0. Unlike the other categories, drowning requires no extended argument to show this; the difference is actually absolute, not merely relative, as 365 people drowned, or were found drowned, in the earlier three years and 310 in the later.

My explanation for this is the same hypothesis suggested by the analyses of casualties and of burns and scalds; people in the earlier period tended to behave more recklessly than those in the later. But it is necessary to explore alternatives that might account, even partially, for the difference in some other way.

The first two alternatives that come to mind must be rejected; there is no evidence that people in 1900 were better swimmers than their predecessors, and although rescue facilities may have improved somewhat, the difference was marginal. One reason for consolidating the city and county in 1854 was to better coordinate the policing of the rivers. By 1870 two harbor police units had long been patrolling the waterfronts. By 1900 the lieutenants in charge were making separate statistical reports and boasted of, among other accomplishments, rescuing four or five watersoaked boatmen each year.[22] But if in fact the rescue service was better than in 1870, the improvement was measured mostly by its exploits *ex post facto;* far more bodies were recovered than revived, and these increased rather than decreased the totals at the health office.

The only factors important enough to have made a substantial difference over time are of a different order—geographical and environmental changes that may have led fewer people to expose themselves to watery hazards in the first place. Philadelphians in the nineteenth century drowned in tubs, vats, ponds, and claypits, and a favored few off Mount Desert. But the overwhelming majority died in the two big rivers, the Delaware, which bounds the city on the east, and the Schuylkill, which after flowing through the west side joins the Delaware to the south. Some victims were working sailors or stevedores, a few ship's passengers, others drunks or children whose falls tumbled them into the water rather than onto the ground. But the great majority were people seeking recreation or relief from the heat. The statistics for drowning by season confirm the count obtained from the newspapers: fishermen, pleasure-boatmen, and above all bathers, young men between fifteen and thirty-five, dominated the totals.

The banks of the Schuylkill remained relatively sylvan throughout the period and almost completely approachable at most points. But the Delaware, in particular, which consistently accounted for more deaths, became somewhat less pleasant and less accessible for recreational use over time.[23] Between 1870 and 1900, however, the construction of Delaware Avenue between Front Street and the docks cut off some casual foot traffic from the bank of the larger river downtown. There were fewer newspaper reports of patrons stumbling out of riverfront "dives" almost directly into the water. And the continual build-up of commercial river traffic, too, may have made swimming and even boating less attractive than in earlier years.

These developments may have "driven" richer residents to the Jersey shore or the coast of Maine to escape the summer heat. But they would not so easily escape the registration rolls. Heavily advertised excursion trains took large numbers of people to Cape May and Atlantic City, and some blades even bicycled down in the 'nineties. But funeral cars took seaside drowning victims back in the other direction; if they were buried in Philadelphia, their certificates were recorded with those of people who had fallen off the docks.

In searching for reasons to account for the decline, the most likely possibility is the proportional movement of the population away from the Delaware. In the old "walking city" of 1840 and earlier, virtually everyone had lived on its eastern curve, within a few blocks of the river. By 1870 this was no longer true, and by 1900 the change was more pronounced. Again, it is impossible to measure the movement precisely, but it occurred and was not fully balanced by the fact that more people lived near the banks of the Schuylkill or the farther northeastern reaches of the Delaware itself. Throughout the period it was customary for people to drink, play games, and sleep out near the water on the city's notoriously hot summer nights. As they moved away, fewer may have taken the trip required, and similarly, fewer may have made the effort by day to get out and enjoy the river directly by swimming, wading, and boating.

The most thickly settled parts of the city were never very far from a river bank; Delaware to Schuylkill, the east-west streets downtown ran for less than thirty blocks. Most of Philadelphia's wards were bounded by one or both rivers. A few, however, were landlocked: five in 1870, twelve in 1900.[24] It is possible to make a rough test for propinquity as a factor in the drowning rate by comparing the rates for these interior wards with those for the city at large.

For 1869-1871, the landlocked rate was 11.8 per 100,000, compared to 18.5 citywide, and in 1899-1901, 6.4 compared to 8.0.[25] But these differences should be further adjusted and narrowed. Some unidentified persons drowned each year, and despite an ice-cooled morgue, erected late in 1870, all drowned persons became physically difficult to identify in time. In these cases the coroner ran a sort of lost-and-found for missing persons, with descriptive notices in the newspapers, seeking to dispose of their bodies as soon as possible—in fact, a regulation had to be passed to restrain him from burying victims within forty-eight hours. The persons who remained unknown were, however, included in the totals by ward, and while it is nowhere stated explicitly, it appears that they were "credited" either to the spot where they were found, to the harbor police stations, or to the morgue itself. Sixty-three people were thus added to the totals for the river wards in 1869-1871, nineteen in 1899-1901. If these were more evenly distributed, the annual rate for the interior wards would be 14.6 for the earlier period, 6.9 for the later.

In short, the somewhat easier access to the water in the earlier period did make some difference but not nearly enough to account for the drop in rates. If the rates of the interior wards alone are compared over time, it is still apparent that proportionately less than half as many people drowned in 1900 as in

1870. And that test may work in another way as well. If the slight difficulty of access did not much discourage the urban teen-agers and young men who dominate the totals *during* 1870 and 1900, then presumably it did not discourage them in the years *between;* as Table 5 shows, they were not discouraged in the previous thirty years, from 1840 to 1870, when the population was also moving away from the river.

There is no clue elsewhere to any change in the nature of people's exposure to the water. In every testable respect it appears that the pattern of use was almost precisely the same, with the same sorts of people visiting the rivers, or at least drowning there, while doing the same sorts of things at the same times of year, which suggests that there was no decrease in the proportion of swimmers as the result of commercial traffic. The seasonal peaks were of course July and August. Perhaps more significant, during the off-season months of December, January, and February, a total of twenty-seven bodies were recovered in 1869-1871, and twenty-four in 1899-1901, or 7.4 percent and 7.7 percent, respectively, of all drowning victims. The age and sex of victims are also much the same in the two periods, certainly more so than in any other class of accident over time. The ratio of male to female deaths in the three years around 1870 was 8.4 to 1, and in the three years around 1900, taking into account the slight increase in the proportion of women in the population, it was 9.8 to 1. In both periods the ratio of those over twenty to those younger was the same—1.2 to 1.

Since changes in the use of water cannot account for the difference any more than changes in geography, the only reasonable explanation for the dropping rate is my original hypothesis: people were behaving differently. Over time there was simply less drunken horseplay on and around the docks and riverbanks, fewer reckless challenges taken, fewer miscalculations made.

The fact that the pattern for all three of the major accident categories turns out to be so similar, on analysis, strengthens the case for each. It requires argument and a chain of inference to discount the impact of technology and establish that pattern for casualties. The argument is less elaborate, and the chain shorter, for burns and scalds. Virtually nothing is required to establish it for drownings. The clarity of the pattern in the last and most obvious case appears to confirm in retrospect the accuracy of the analysis in the first and least obvious. And the explanation is comprehensive as well; whether at work, at home, or at play, the people of Philadelphia were typically becoming more careful, more sober, perhaps even more rational in their everyday habits and activities, at least during the last thirty years of the century.

CHAPTER 4

HOMICIDE: I

Homicide is statistically the least significant of the forms of violent death. Less common, or less commonly counted, than suicide and far less common than accident, it was also in some senses less representative of life in nineteenth-century Philadelphia. Although the other two forms of death were at least reasonably, if not evenly, distributed through the ranks of social class, homicide with some striking exceptions was concentrated among low-status or even marginal people and groups.[1] But in spite of these limitations, the records and accounts of murder are an important source of social history.

The first trial brought before the Court of Oyer and Terminer in 1839 arose from the killing of Eliza Sowers of Manayunk.[2] A few months earlier Miss Sowers, a girl of twenty, had been working in Eckstein's Mill while awaiting marriage to an "honest lover" from Norristown, just upriver. Late in May she took a less strenuous job as a domestic in the family of her supervisor, William Nixon, a man later accused of forcing his attentions on several of the women in his employ. Eliza became pregnant late that month or early the next, but she did not confide in either family or friends. In September she felt obliged to break her engagement; a sister recalled her tearfully telling the young man that she was "unworthy" of him. On October 3 she left on a mysterious errand in Philadelphia; Saturday night, October 13, Nixon and a Dr. Henry Chauncey arrived at her home to tell the family she had died of "impacted bowels," producing a death certificate signed by a second physician, one William Armstrong. The girl's brothers met this message, and the messengers, with angry skepticism and demanded an exhumation. The resultant evidence of abortion by a steel instrument led to the indictment of Dr. Chauncey as principal, Nixon and Armstrong as accessories.

The trial was bitter. The defense team, having little positive evidence, concentrated on damning the girl, the family, and the chief prosecution witness, a Mrs. Mary Kingsley, in whose infamous establishment some sort of operation had clearly taken place. They contended that the "honest lover" had been the real seducer; that the witnesses were of an untrustworthy class; that the abortion had been induced by Eliza herself, drinking noxious substances made of oil of tansy, pennyroyal, and other weeds; that Dr. Chauncey had merely assisted, out of charity, in removing the afterbirth. Despite the presence of crowds outside the court, who threatened to lynch the three defendants, these arguments created enough reasonable doubt to win acquittal for Nixon and Armstrong and a mere malpractice verdict against Chauncey. One week afterward the *Public Ledger* announced that D. Paul Brown, Esq., member of the defense team and the leading criminal lawyer in the city, would again deliver his favorite lecture at the Musical Fund Hall. The subject was "Shakespeare, His Writings, Etc. Revised and Retouched"; proceeds would go to the Society for Meliorating the Condition of Impecunious Laboring Females.

Manayunk, still a mill town within the boundaries of the city, was also the scene of another crime, very different from this Early Victorian Tragedy, which resulted in the last murder indictment issued in 1901. On December 3 of that year, Dominic Venezial accused his landlord, a fellow immigrant named Virgilio Detriro, of stealing twenty dollars from a trunk; that night Detriro shot Venezial as he slept.[3] Since this was the first case tried by a new and eager district attorney, it was pressed with unusual vigor and resulted in an unusually hard verdict of murder in the first degree. This was overturned on appeal, and a new trial granted; in March the defendant pleaded guilty to second-degree murder and drew fifteen years in the Eastern State Penitentiary. Confinement in the prison either aggravated or precipitated insanity, however, and the following summer, on advice of a court-appointed panel of physicians, Detriro was transferred to the state asylum at Norristown.

Homicide, as these examples indicate, always reflects in some way the society in which it occurs, as does its treatment by the law, the courts, and the press. As with suicide and accident, the first step in analyzing the issues raised is to establish an index and assess its reliability and direction, the purpose of this chapter. Then in the next it becomes possible to compare nineteenth-century homicides in Philadelphia with those of the late twentieth. In both chapters the fact that the available information is so much fuller than for other forms of violence makes it uniquely possible to go beyond the incidence of homicide into a more fruitful investigation of changing subgroups and differing circumstances over time.

13 Commonwealth	May 15th 1839. 1 count Murder
V.	1 count Involuntary Manslaughter.
George Force	True Bill as to 2 count
	Ignoramus on the 1st count.
	Continued til next term, defendent
	and John Force tent. in 500.00 that
	dft appear at next court of Oyer
	and Term.
	May 20th 1839 the defendent being
	arr. pleads guilty
	May 22d 1841. Def't sentenced by
	the Court of General Sessions to
	pay a fine of one dollar and costs
	of prosecution.
	Docket Book of Court of Oyer
	and Terminer, May term, 1839

The figures for nineteenth-century murder are more difficult to compile than those for the twentieth. Modern criminologists have generally sought to measure the incidence of homicide by arrest rates, following the rule that criminal statistics are most reliable when the source is closest in time to the event; the machinery of justice has a way of filtering cases out of the record during the long passage between perpetration and disposition.[4] Criminologists have also regarded homicide statistics as one of the firmest indices of "real" criminal activity or violence, because they are relatively immune to problems of definition or to changes in the level of social tolerance as reflected in public policy.

For the study of homicide in an earlier period, however, these axioms do not hold, for several reasons, beginning with the fact that the usual sources are not usually the best, and others must be sought. It is neither possible nor desirable to use police arrest figures as an index. In Philadelphia, as elsewhere in this country, a modern police force developed gradually during the three decades before the Civil War, but modern record-keeping lagged some years behind, so that the first annual report of arrests dates only from 1857. Even when available, this is a poor barometer of the incidence of homicide, not only for the reasons common to all official sources—the unknowable number of undetected cases—but for others peculiar to police practice in the previous century. Some accused murderers, as discussed below, were never processed by the police. More commonly, in homicides resulting from brawls and those of great notoriety, the force resorted to dragnet procedures that greatly magnified the arrest totals. As a result the superintendent in Philadelphia could report a total of six homicide arrests for all of 1869, and eighteen for the month of April, 1870.

An even better index in theory, the equivalent of the modern record of "crimes known to the police," would be the coroner's list of inquest verdicts, but these reports are available for only a few years. The health office figures for homicide, which are largely based upon the coroner's records, proved unreliable because of a legal-bureaucratic quirk in the registration process. Tabulated from death certificates signed by the coroner, the health office figures were in every case lower than those from any other source. For the seventeen years in which both sets of figures are available, they were cumulatively 32 percent lower than the coroner's annual totals, a discrepancy that apparently resulted from the differing purposes of the two offices.

In most cases the verdict of a coroner's jury was phrased in one to three words, "apoplexy" or "mania-a-potu," which fitted easily on a death certificate. A homicide, however, required a short descriptive essay: thus Louisia Franklin, "W/F 45," died of "compression of the brain the result of falling from a chair while intoxicated said fall was caused by a slap in the face at the hands of Michael Leonard at 422 Callowhill St. July 7, 1879."[5] In editing these for registration purposes, the coroner had a great deal of latitude in deciding which "facts" were relevant. His own responsibility was legal, because in homicide cases the full verdicts went to the clerk of the Court of Quarter Sessions. The health office, however, was concerned not with forensic but with physical medicine. In 1885, for example, in the case of a white male, thirty, who died after having a leg amputated, the result of a brawl, the jury sought to fix responsibility for the fight.[6] But the *Annual Register of Deaths* listed the cause of death as simply "Bright's disease," which contemporary physicians understood as traumatic as well as chronic renal failure, and which for scientific purposes was perhaps the most pertinent information.

In the years for which a crosscheck is possible, there is a pattern to those cases in which the coroner omitted any indication of homicide in spite of inquest verdicts to that effect. The notation does not appear in cases of poisoning or of obvious self-defense, or one in which a streetcar conductor threw an obnoxious drunk off the train and under the wheels. When a stranger was found in April 1878 with his throat cut "by a person or persons to this jury unknown" the certificate simply reads "W/M 55—ruptured aortic valve."[7]

This pattern in turn seems related to a second; although the health office totals are consistently lower than those for arrests, inquest verdicts, and other sources, toward the end of the century at least they are remarkably similar to those of the annual record of court convictions. The reason is not entirely clear, but it seems that the coroner's fee system encouraged a kind of speculation on the outcome of murder trials, so that the number of homicides reported to the health office was as close to the number of guilty verdicts as a shrewd coroner could guess. As had been true in England, all inquest costs were borne by the county, except in cases of homicide, when they were chargeable to the accused slayer.[8] "Costs" were generally included in the sentence of a convicted killer. While it is hard to imagine that the fees were easily squeezed out of their estates, that was undoubtedly easier than trying to collect from an indignant man who had won an acquittal.

In any case, once the health office figures have been discounted, only one satisfactory measure of homicide remains: the number of indictments prepared for the grand juries each year. Fortunately this is a very useful index and, not simply by default, one that fulfills all of the relevant criteria for any official source.[9] Indictments are available for all the years covered in this study. Unlike arrests or coroners' figures, which are merely totals, they are full entries, providing essential information about individual cases, as in the example that heads this section. And they are, after inquest verdicts, as close to the starting point in the chain of criminal procedure as any record can be.

The first step was the coroner's inquest, the most important filter in the system of processing homicides. Some cases of course escaped an inquest entirely, and in others the jurors returned a verdict other than murder; together these make up the "dark figure" for crimes that never find their way into any official series. After the inquest verdict was forwarded to the courts, the next step was the preparation of an indictment by the district attorney. With the exception of the relatively few verdicts involving "a person or persons unknown to this jury," those in which a suspect died in the interval (at most a few weeks) between death of the victim and preparation of the bill, and those that with court permission were dropped at this early stage, these indictments include all the homicides found by the coroner. They also include some for which no arrests were made, as when a known suspect escaped, and several in which arrests were not recorded by the police force, as when the coroner himself bound a suspect over to the grand jury, calling on the sheriff to take him into custody. The indictments were recorded before the cases reached the next major filter, the actual hearing before the Grand Jury of Philadelphia County. Thus, while each indictment embodies a judgment of an inquest jury and the district attorney that a criminal killing had occurred, the total includes a number of cases that the grand jury later determined should not be tried or could not be tried successfully; the docket entry in such cases reads simply "ignoramus" rather than "true bill."

As in the previous chapters, the years 1839 to 1901 are divided into nine intervals; the rates of indictment for murder and manslaughter in each period are shown in Table 8.[10] The long-term trend is clearly, if erratically, downward. But as with other indices, the raw figures require further analysis before yielding significant information. Much like accidents, homicides were affected by changes in technology; far more than suicides, surprisingly, they were affected by changes in official policy. The effect of each factor must be considered in turn.

> I heard Gallagher say to Madden "You are a sucker." Gallagher then grabbed a glass and threw it at Mr. Madden. McDonough also threw a glass. Mr. Geary made a grab for the men and then I heard a shot and Geary fell. Mr. Madden and Geary were good friends.
>
> Testimony in *Commonweath Vs. Joseph Madden*, in *Coroner's Evidence Book*, September 19, 1876

The modal homicide in nineteenth-century Philadelphia resulted from a brawl or quarrel originating in a saloon but reaching a climax in the street. Drink was an important part of the culture of the city, enormously so among those subgroups in which most killings occurred; as in Western cultures generally, drunkenness was closely associated with assault. Other than the alcohol itself, whatever allegedly precipitated the trouble—a spilled drink, a careless remark, an argument

Table 8.   Number and average annual rate per 100,000 population of
incidents resulting in homicide indictments, by period.

Years	No.	7-yr. rate	No.	21-yr. rate
1839-1845	73	3.7		
1846-1852	85	3.1		
1853-1859	138	4.0	296	3.6
1860-1866	100	2.4		
1867-1873	156	3.3		
1874-1880	205	3.7	461	3.2
1881-1887	159	2.4		
1888-1894	167	2.2		
1895-1901	231	2.7	557	2.5

Source: See appendix B.

about the merits of different steam engines—almost always
seemed tragically out of proportion to the aftermath.

Perhaps, as in the case of Big John Rox, fighting for its own
sake served a recreational function or, cumulatively, an instrumental one, to the extent that a reputation for toughness was a
social or even economic asset. But the price was high. Rox was a
figure out of the heroic age of Irish immigration, before the
Great Famine, a powerful man who had apparently parlayed
his brute strength into a position as labor contractor and owner
of a small string of taverns. Convicted of manslaughter in May
1839 for killing his old friend "Pat" Kelly with an axhandle, he
was pardoned by the governor in time to get involved in a similar episode just twelve months later.[11] He and Barney Browning, his closest surviving companion, were quarreling in Gunn's
Tavern about who had been the toughest man in Donegal,
where both had grown up, when Rox confirmed his claim by
beating the smaller man onto the floor with his fists. At the bar
just afterward, much subdued, he turned occasionally to the
dying Browning and urged him to stop "playing possum" and
join in a few more rounds. These befuddled appeals dramatize
the element of disproportion or impulsiveness that marked hundreds of such episodes over the next sixty years. What distin-

guishes it from many in later years was the absence of gunplay.

Throughout the century, Philadelphians used firearms of all kinds to kill each other, but until the introduction of Samuel Colt's revolver and its copies, this use was relatively limited.[12] The older single-shot pistols—dueling or military weapons too bulky to be hidden on the person—were little better adapted to routine use in the city than rifles or shotguns. It was not until the 1850s that concealed weapons and an increase in shootings among the "dangerous classes" became a matter of concern.

Even then pocket pistols remained expensive, their possession for many years confined perhaps to the most troubled, and troublesome, elements in the population. Two well-known chroniclers of the urban elite, Sidney George Fisher in Philadelphia and George Templeton Strong in New York, mentioned in the decade before the Civil War that frightened gentlemen were beginning to go armed.[13] City police forces also began to carry revolvers, unofficially until the early 1860s but in many cases officially thereafter. Both gentlemen and police were reacting to the increased firepower commanded by young toughs, members of street gangs and fire companies, political plug-uglies and criminals. The figures for suicide in chapter 2, however, imply that handguns were as yet not common among ordinary citizens. Suicidal persons, although in some sense troubled by definition, were not normally troublesome to those concerned with the state of public order, and it was not until some time between 1857 and the early 1880s that firearms became a leading means of self-destruction. The most authoritative recent study finds further that it was not until the 1880s or 1890s that mass production of two-dollar "suicide specials" eliminated "the last modest economic restraints to pistol ownership."[14] Although not so common as in the late twentieth century, revolvers were then available to all.

There is no question that the practice of carrying handguns affected the murder rate. This is partly confirmed by the figures in Table 9 on the proportion of homicides involving firearms. But the table, as so many others, requires further explanation. The figure given for 1839-1845 is somewhat misleading. Of the nine homicides by firearms reported, six resulted from a single

Table 9.   Percentages of all homicides tried in which the murder weapon was a firearm, by period.

Years	Percentage	Years	Percentage
1839-1845	19	1874-1880	29
1846-1852	13	1881-1887	27
1853-1859	25	1888-1894	22
1860-1866	23	1895-1901	21
1867-1873	33		

Source: See appendix B.

series of incidents, the great anti-Catholic Kensington Riots of 1844, which involved several thousand participants and ultimately brought out the militia. Two of these killings were further atypical in that the weapons, listed with perfect logic under "firearms," were in fact cannon. This group aside, most of the gun killings for the fourteen years through 1852 involved some degree of premeditation, as a husband seeking out and murdering an estranged and errant wife, or the protection of home or property from some perceived threat. With two exceptions, in 1849 and 1852, there were no gun-killing incidents arising impulsively from quarrels. It was during the next period, from 1853 through 1859, that the revolver multiplied the deadly potential in barroom brawls and street fights.

In theory the growing practice of carrying guns might have raised the flash point at which debate or annoyance erupted physically, as rational calculation of the consequences might persuade a man to avoid offense. In practice the circumstances do not suggest that rational calculation was anywhere at work in most alcoholic encounters, and if some were intimidated into prudence, it appears that others, with pistols in their pockets, were tempted into imprudence. Whatever the emotional temperature at which an explosion took place, it was the events following which were transformed by the presence of a revolver, and over time an incalculable number of people were murdered in circumstances that earlier might have led to nothing more serious than a drunken pushing match.

During 1853-1859 in twenty of the ninety-three incidents that came to trial, it seems wholly unlikely that death would have resulted if guns had not been available instantly. Most of these were bar or street fights, but there were other sorts of trouble, also, that had not often proved lethal in previous years. Violent rivalries among volunteer fire companies had been a source of official concern for some time, because deaths sometimes resulted from their riotous encounters and ambuscades. The presence of small arms, however, encouraged escalation, and there were three trials for shooting firemen between 1854 and 1859. The period also witnessed a parallel "first" in killings by armed police. Early in the century an arrest by a peace officer could degenerate at any time into a bloody mutual assault, but for the first fifteen years of this study no such incident resulted in a trial for homicide. But the consolidation of city and county in 1854, largely inspired by elite fears for public safety, was followed immediately by the creation of a full-time professional corps of police. Although not officially armed, the new officers shot four men to death, over the next five years, under circumstances that the district attorney considered triable. Less dramatic but equally significant for the future, in 1856 and 1857 ordinary domestic battles between husband and wife were ended with bullets, the first two in another series that stretched and grew into the next century.

After the crucial middle 1850s, the rates of homicide were not so dramatically affected by the use of small arms. As Table 9 shows, a peak was reached shortly after the Civil War, and then the proportion slowly declined. But this fact is itself significant in determining the kind of behavior that lay behind the rates. The large number of indictments between 1839 and 1852 seems especially large given the general lack of firearms; it is easy to imagine that it might have been significantly higher if guns had been more available. Conversely, the falling homicide rate late in the century appears the more remarkable when measured against the increasing cheapness and hence rising availability of pocket pistols. Either men felt less need to own and carry them, or they were learning to control their tempers.

> Quite a large mob was collected yesterday, in Arch Street,
> above Ninth—one of the most quiet parts of the city—by a
> really dreadful fight between two men. The parties only
> ceased from exhaustion, arising from loss of blood. One of
> the belligerents had his nose bitten off, and both were del-
> uged with blood . . .
>
> *Public Ledger,* November 26, 1840

While the introduction of the revolver had an important impact on the "real" rate of homicide, changes in the practice of criminal justice affected only the rates officially recorded. But an understanding of these changes is at least equally important in making meaningful comparisons over time. Changing standards of prosecution reveal more about the social transformation of the city than does anything so simple as the advance of the urban gun culture. Specifically these standards help illumine how the socially acceptable level of, or threshold of tolerance for, violence was changing as the century progressed.

The interpretation of criminal statistics is always difficult. Many series suggest at least two opposite possibilities, and the most common error is simply to take the literal reading without considering and testing for any other. Especially with common offenses such as gambling and drunkenness, a high or rising number of arrests may mean a high or rising incidence of the behavior. But it may also mean, and often did mean in nineteenth-century American cities, a lowered threshold of tolerance, a change in official policy accompanying, indeed enabled by, a decline in the number of offenses committed.[15] Rising arrests, in many categories, may then be taken as an index of an increasing demand for public order or perhaps of increasing faith in the judicial system. A warrant for assault and battery is, after all, a highly civilized alternative to a reciprocal fist in the face.

Homicide, along with a few other serious crimes, constitutes a special case. There is no incalculable pool of murderers, as there is of drunks or gamblers, from which the authorities may more or less arbitrarily pull out and "label" offenders as criminal, nor is the area of discretion as wide as with assault or larceny. But even murder, upon examination, is in part a matter of definition. And as with other crimes, the meanings assigned by legal experts and professionals are ultimately governed by the level of social tolerance.

Neither the definition of nor the statutory punishment for the varieties of homicide changed substantially during the nineteenth century. By an act of 1794, the Commonwealth of Pennsylvania was the first of the new American states to confine capital punishment to persons convicted of murder in the first degree.[16] The general criminal code was revised twice in the following century, in 1829 and 1860; the commissioners in 1860 wrote simply that since the original act, "This law has been so thoroughly considered, and its construction and meaning so entirely settled by a long course of judicial decision, that they have deemed it inexpedient to make any important alteration thereof."[17]

First-degree murder, accordingly, was defined as homicide committed in the course of a major felony or involving premeditation; the penalty was hanging, always. Murder in the second degree was interpreted as a crime in which "a felonious and malicious homicide is committed, but without a specific attempt to take life"; the intent might be only to maim or injure, and drunkenness was often sufficient defense against the charge of premeditation.

Voluntary manslaughter was homicide in which "the circumstances must negative all evidence of cool depravity of heart, or of wanton cruelty," as when two people "agreed" to fight, or a third party was inadvertently but fatally injured. Involuntary manslaughter was legally held to occur when no major injury was intended at all, but the accused was involved in "some unlawful act not amounting to felony; or an act not strictly unlawful in itself, but done in an unlawful manner, and without due caution," as in accidents involving firearms or collisions in traffic. The range of punishments for all but first-degree murder was slightly lowered in 1829, and in 1860 the new code for most offenses prescribed maximum sentences only, allowing judges to set minimums at their discretion. The limit for second-degree murder and for manslaughter was set at twelve years, for involuntary manslaughter at two. The legal definitions remained as before.

Actual practice in the courts, however, was shaped by the

continuing battle between trial juries and district attorneys. The key distinction was the one between murder and manslaughter, and the latter term in particular was stretched to cover a great variety of situations, as prosecutors pulled one way and jurors another. Virtually all killings sparked by ill will or anger, however briefly it may have flared, were indicted as "murder," without distinction of degree. Although in the course of a trial the prosecution might indicate that a finding of murder in the second degree would be appropriate, the decision was generally left to be clarified by the judge and settled by the jury. The most common verdict in these cases, if guilt was found at all, was, however, manslaughter, no matter what the indictment read and, within limits, no matter what the facts of the case. Original indictments for manslaughter, on the other hand, as though prosecutors were determined to compensate for this lenience, were generally reserved for cases of accident, in which the accused had clearly intended no harm at all but had shot a friend in a fit of careless exuberance ("Hear My Bulldog Bark!") or had run down a stranger with a carriage. Involuntary manslaughter was almost always included as a secondary charge in these indictments; when used as the sole charge, it apparently distinguished some lesser shade of moral guilt without definable legal basis, the difference perhaps between driving too fast and driving much too fast.

During the century as a whole, the rate of conviction in all homicide cases was quite low. Juries, especially early in the period, were usually quite tolerant of assaultive behavior and were always greatly influenced by moral or social rather than purely legal considerations. Especially because so many killings were committed without weapons, juries were often faced with a situation in which the accused killer might be regarded as the loser in a kind of lottery. In these cases murder was surely, in James Q. Wilson's phrase, nothing more than "successful assault."[18] Out of thousands of blows struck in anger, a few found their way to sensitive spots, bringing to the dock a man only somewhat less unlucky than his victim. Again and again doctors argued successfully that the blow or even wound would not have killed a "healthy" man or woman—or, even better, a "temperate" one.

The plea of self-defense was even stronger in law and more common in practice. Nearly 84 percent of those accused of murder and 87 percent of those accused of manslaughter pleaded innocent, although there was rarely any doubt that they had been involved in some sort of affray with those they were accused of killing. In 1860 the commissioners in charge of revising the criminal code were forced to recognize the problem that "the law, in its anxiety for the protection of human life, has held many homicides to be manslaughters where the killing has taken place under circumstances approximating the crime very near homicides in self-defense."[19] The resultant reform, which as noted allowed judges to set minimum penalties as low as they pleased and to substitute in some cases "simple imprisonment" for "imprisonment at hard labor," was part of a general strategy designed to increase the rate of conviction.[20]

The percentage of indicted persons convicted in murder cases did slowly rise over time, as indicated in Table 10. In part the rising rate represents an increased assertiveness by the office of district attorney. Prosecutors over time learned either to present technically stronger cases or to dominate grand juries, as indicated by the decreasing number of cases ignored. More accused murderers were brought to the dock, and fewer indictments were nol-prossed, quashed, or otherwise lost in the stage between the finding of a true bill and arraignment in court. As the century progressed, the increasing number of guilty pleas, most of which represented bargaining arrangements with the defense for a lesser charge or sentence, also helped to improve the rate of successful prosecution. These developments do not mean, however, that the cases brought to trial were inherently stronger toward the end of the century than they had been earlier; indeed the very reverse seems true. The fundamental difference was that the men called to serve on the petit jury, the mechanism through which the middle classes helped shape the operation of the justice system, were becoming less tolerant of violence.

This lowering of the threshold may be demonstrated in several ways. If murder indictments alone are considered, there was relatively little difference over time in the percentage of persons convicted of the various degrees of homicide. But there was a

Table 10.   Disposition of first-degree murder indictments, by period.

Years	No. indict-ments	No. not tried[1]	No. tried	No. Convicted		% of in-dicted who were con-victed
				Plea	Jury	
1839-1845	68	28	40	0	25	37
1846-1852	77	19	57	3	30	43
1853-1859	126	32	93	1	40	33
1860-1866	96	18	78	1	36	39
1867-1873	150	18	130	1	62	42
1874-1880	149	21	125	5	58	42
1881-1887	145	8	137	27	41	47
1888-1894	172	10	160	64	27	53
1895-1901	215	9	201	58	34	63

Source: See appendix B. Includes all persons to limit of 3 per case.
1. Includes cases nol-prossed or quashed by the prosecution and those ig-nored by the grand jury. Because of death, escape, or error, there may be slight discrepancies in the totals.

notable increase in the harshness of the penalties, the proportion sentenced to death or to more than twelve years in prison, as indicated in Table 11.

But changing attitudes are most clearly demonstrated by the changing treatment of manslaughter, as indicated in Table 12. These lesser charges were usually brought only in cases of accident, as explained above. Involuntary manslaughter was rarely used as a principal accusation at any time and never appeared more than once or twice in any year. The charge of voluntary manslaughter, while not common until the 1870s, was brought fairly often from that time on. The increase cannot be attributed to the technological developments described in chapter 3 that accounted for an increasing proportion of fatal casualties. Few manslaughter incidents involved machinery of any kind; most of those that were brought to court were the result of traffic collisions or of carelessness in tending fires, mixing medicines, or playing with guns—problems that were on the whole decreasing rather than increasing in incidence. Just twenty-one cases, in

Table 11.   Convictions and sentences in first-degree murder cases, by 21-year period.

Years	No. convicted	% manslaughter or less	% 1st deg.	% 2nd deg.
1839-1859	99	45	40	14
1860-1880	163	40	43	18
1881-1901	251	47	38	15

Years	No. sentenced[1]	% sentenced to 12 yrs. or less	% more than 12 yrs.	% death
1839-1859	95	82	5	12
1860-1880	151	76	8	16
1881-1901	231	71	16	13

Source: See appendix B. Includes all persons to limit of 3 per case.
1. It is impossible to tell how much of the discrepancy between number convicted and number sentenced is due to death, to error, or to suspension.

Table 12.   Disposition of manslaughter indictments, by period.

Years	Indictments	Tried	Convicted
1839-1845	6	3	1
1846-1852	10	6	3
1853-1859	12	5	4
1860-1866	5	0	0
1867-1873	9	6	3
1874-1880	62	54	13
1881-1887	20	16	6
1888-1894	9	8	3
1895-1901	46	43	18

Source: See appendix B. Includes all persons to limit of 3 per case.

two periods, 1875-1878 and 1895-1897, can apparently be attributed to a change in policy. During parts of those six years, uniquely, prosecutors seemed to bend with rather than overcompensate for the sentiments of juries by using the voluntary manslaughter charge in something close to its lawbook sense, to cover homicides resulting from flash fights in which no weapons were used. But except for those years the increase in these indictments resulted mostly from prosecutorial aggressiveness, a lowered threshold, a determination to punish in·cases that had earlier been ignored—considered unfortunate but not truly blameworthy.

The figures in Table 8, then, need to be revised. That table includes all episodes resulting in indictments for homicide, including both murder and manslaughter. It thus includes a number of incidents in which no assault, aggression, or harm was intended. Table 13 omits these accidents and includes indictments only for murder and those twenty-one more strictly defined cases of manslaughter; now the slope changes in a way that more nearly reflects the changing level of interpersonal violence in the city.

Although Table 13 is closer to reality, it still considerably understates the decline in the homicide rate. When examined case by case, the indictments for murder reveal a further stretching of definitions, a changing appraisal of what constituted a punishable offense and in what degree. When the beginning, the middle, and the end of the whole period 1839 to 1901 are compared, the differences in practice, while they cannot be quantified, are often clearer than the statistical differences.

During the three years 1839-1841, twenty-nine indictments were issued for murder. Those persons brought to trial were correctly charged with murder, by any definition, with two possible exceptions. The second offense committed by John Rox, described earlier, and one other incident, a stomping, might be classified as manslaughter. In all of the rest, weapons were used, guns in three cases, a variety of instruments sharp or blunt in the others. Five murder indictments were ignored by the grand jury, apparently for prudential reasons; in any criminal proceeding for violence, the odds were against conviction,

Table 13. Number and average annual rate per 100,000 population of
non-accidental incidents resulting in homicide indictments,
by period.

Years	No.	7-yr. rate	No.	21-yr. rate
1839-1845	67	3.4		
1846-1852	75	2.7		
1853-1859	126	3.6	268	3.3
1860-1866	95	2.3		
1867-1873	147	3.1		
1874-1880	159	2.9	401	2.8
1881-1887	139	2.1		
1888-1894	158	2.1		
1895-1901	190	2.2	487	2.1

Source: See appendix B.

and these five cases seemed especially weak.[21] Two of them
were infanticides; in another the victim was a visiting New
Yorker in a whorehouse, and the madam and a male associate
were indicted simply for lack of other suspects; in the fourth a
white man from upstate, after stabbing a local black, had
skipped bail and disappeared by the time the panel reached the
case. The fifth was a charge of manslaughter, unaccountably,
for a stabbing, which for equally unaccountable reasons was ignored. No indictments of any kind were issued for accidental
killings in those three years.

Of the remaining cases, two involved minors, boys, and were
accordingly handled with tolerance. In February 1839 fourteen-
year-old George Quain was working in a pencil-box factory
high above the street in Franklin Place; during a lunch break he
saw a number of other boys doing battle on a lot below and
threw a brick into the hostilities.[22] This foolish and perhaps vi-
cious action fractured the skull of Francis Gilles, a twelve-year-
old immigrant employed as a waiter. Quain was indicted in an
unusual fashion; the first charge was murder; the second, not
voluntary but involuntary manslaughter. This device enabled
the grand jury to ignore the first charge, and the district attorney to proceed with the second. After several delays Quain

pleaded guilty, then innocent, eventually receiving a suspended sentence. In May of the same year young George Force (age not specified) fatally stabbed John G. Andrews in the groin.[23] His father had to stand bail, but the boy, like Quain, went through a routine in which a murder charge was ignored and only a secondary accusation of involuntary manslaughter was pressed, and lightly. After pleading guilty, Force was fined one dollar and costs.

Thirty years later, a more complicated series of homicide incidents was handled according to standards somewhat more severe but basically similar to those of 1839-1841. In 1870 a total of twenty-three incidents resulted in murder indictments against thirty-five individuals. Only one man was held for an accident: Adolph Fisher, a German immigrant who had drunkenly driven his wagon into a ninety-year-old woman and then compounded his offense by riding away.[24] The grand jury ignored the murder charge; Fisher was tried for voluntary manslaughter, convicted of involuntary manslaughter, recommended to the mercy of the court, and fined. Of the murder cases that came to trial, perhaps seven, none of them involving weapons, might have been prosecuted as manslaughter. Seven others were ignored. Three of these resulted from a single brawl in which the prosecution decided that it was impossible to distinguish who was guilty of what, and one involved the killing of a fireman under equally smoky conditions. The rest of the ignored indictments occurred when two or more were held in a single killing, and it was decided to prosecute only the most surely or obviously guilty. Only two persons under eighteen were indicted, fifteen-year-old Mike Walsh and seventeen-year-old James Donnelly.[25] One or both of them had broken the neck of young Sam Simes in the course of a two-on-two battle over who owed how much money to whom; the bill against Donnelly was ignored, and Walsh was sentenced to two years for manslaughter.

By the turn of the century, definitions had changed more drastically. During 1900 twenty-eight incidents resulted in murder indictments, five in voluntary manslaughter, one in concealing the death of a bastard child, and one in involuntary manslaughter. All of the voluntary manslaughter cases were accidents. The concealment charge was clearly a prosecutorial attempt, and a successful one, to get around the notorious difficulty in convicting a single woman for infanticide.[26] The involuntary manslaughter indictment resulted from a more complicated case, which, in its different standards for dealing with juveniles, suggests something more general about the changing threshold of tolerance for violence.

On April 23 eleven-year-old Palmer Berry swallowed a tin whistle as a result of a bump or shove by an even younger playmate.[27] Earlier that year the coroner, Michael Dugan, had refused to agree to the indictment of eight-year-old Pauline Yeager for fatally hitting a playmate with a scrub brush, instead releasing her in her mother's custody with a strict warning.[28] On August 8 he ordered the release of Samuel Shetzline, also eight years old, who had been committed to Moyamensing Prison in the death of James Dever, twelve, several days after a fist fight.[29] An inquest jury ruled that Dever had died of spinal meningitis; there were few injuries, and in any case, as Dugan pointed out, the older boy had been the aggressor. After six-year-old James Doudy died on September 27, his relatives sought charges against a schoolmate who had struck him the preceding April![30] Dugan resisted that notion and presided over an inquest in which it was declared that James had died of scarlet fever. No demands for prosecutions of this kind had publicly been voiced in either 1839-1841 or in 1870, and no preadolescents had been tried in either era. But several times, late in the century, young children were booked for homicide.[31] And in the Berry incident the coroner believed and declared that ten-year-old Bertram Van Horn was "a bad boy." As a result this case went to the district attorney and through a grand jury, before twelve adult males finally decided that the push had been more bump than shove, and young Van Horn went free.

The circumstances of several of the 1900 murder indictments are equally significant. On May 13 a high-speed crash totally destroyed a railroad engine, instantly killing its fireman, William Hinchman. It was not until the next day that the *Ledger* reported the discovery of what were "believed to be parts of the body of" Edward Lash, the engineer. A signalman, William

Lantrell, was arrested in the incident, and the grand jury in June approved two indictments charging him with murder.[32] No malice was alleged.

During the same month an unemployed sailor, James Gowan, was indicted for murder in the death of his aged mother.[33] It was clear that Sarah Gowan had hanged herself, and the coroner's jury had so ruled. But Gowan's apparent indifference, the general disorder of their joint household, and a history of mutual ill will combined to make a bad impression, and the district attorney was moved to charge that he had "driven" the old woman to taking her life.

The same grand jury managed finally to ignore a bill for murder brought against ten-year-old Frank Dougherty, perhaps because he had been rushed before them in convulsions, a reaction to confinement without bail in Moyamensing Prison.[34] Dougherty was accused of having pushed another ten-year-old, Nelson Mowatt, off the banks of the Schuylkill nearly a year earlier, on August 23, 1899. At that time an inquest had cleared him, partly because Mowatt's mother testified that the incident was accidental. The woman had since changed her mind and had come to believe that Frank had killed her son out of rivalry for the affections of her employer, Henry Magilton, a kindly old gentleman who was wont to shower the boys with mandolins and bicycles.

Three months later the September grand jury found true bills for murder against two odd young men, Henry Sollenburger and Ezra Sheils, in the death of a baby who had been committed to their care. The two had recently arrived from the Middle West to set up a "Fire-Baptized Holiness Mission" in the city.[35] In addition to a storefront church, they operated a "Beulah Orphanage" for children referred by members of their small flock. One of the inmates, seven-month-old Edward Hacks, died of cholera infantum late in the summer. But when the case came to official attention, the ill-fed condition of the other "orphans" and the fact that no doctor had been called—the missionaries did not believe in conventional medicine—resulted in proceedings for murder.

The same September panel also heard a case that generated

more indictments than any other in the century. It was set in motion on the afternoon of June 17, when an explosion in a one-room fireworks factory in South Philadelphia killed two immigrant workmen. After Coroner Dugan seized some of the torpedoes as evidence for the inquest, the owner, Frank Di Genna, won them back on a writ of replevin. It was later alleged, however, that the writ had been granted only on the unwritten understanding that the seized explosives be taken out of state, as too dangerous for sale in the city. In fact Di Genna turned them over on consignment to his friend and neighbor Antonio Marmorello, who owned a small grocery at 755 South Eighth Street. Marmorello put them in a box outside the store. And on the morning of July 4, in the midst of a crowded and noisy sidewalk celebration, Isaac Harris, a twelve-year-old black youngster, shot a toy pistol into what he thought was an empty box. The resultant explosion killed nine children and sent nine more to the hospital, including Harris. Two months later, as a further result, twenty-seven murder indictments were approved against Marmorello, Di Genna—two of whose daughters were among the victims—and young Harris, to whom the warrants were served in bed. In October these were followed by twenty-seven more, accusing the three of voluntary and involuntary manslaughter as well.[36]

In the end these cases and those cited earlier—eight of the twenty-eight for which homicide indictments were drawn in 1900—did not run the full course. Harris and Marmorello were freed on all counts; Di Genna, after twenty minutes of jury deliberation, drew three months on the lowest. Sheils and Sollenburger got similar sentences for manslaughter. Gowan and Lantrell were declared not guilty; Dougherty's case, as noted, never reached trial. But every incident except the last had passed through two or three procedural filters, as murder, before reaching a petit jury. None of the cases was unprecedented; close parallels can be found for the overzealousness displayed in each. But the earliest of these parallels—a trial for murder in a hit-and-run driving case—dated only from 1879. All such indictments were products of the changing standards of the late century years.

In sum, then, the best set of homicide statistics available for Philadelphia in the last century is the record of indictments drawn. These figures indicate a drop in the incidence of murder and manslaughter over time, but without adjustment and more careful definition they tend to underestimate the real rate of change. The index was falling despite two important contrary tendencies: the increasing availability of firearms and a lowering of the threshold of tolerance for violence. The effect of the first, which made homicide more easy, is to intensify the significance of the finding that homicide was occurring less often. The effect of the second is to misrepresent the downward slope of the index, because late in the century a number of cases were prosecuted that earlier would have been tolerated or overlooked. Thus the actual slope should be more steep than it appears.

With the direction established, what remains is to compare the patterns of nineteenth-century homicide with those of the late twentieth century.

CHAPTER 5

HOMICIDE: II

The means of effecting a comparison between one age and
another, in their criminal and social aspects, cannot be
found in sufficient abundance in printed books.

Luke Owen Pike,
A History of Crime in England

Despite the differences outlined in chapter 4, the
years 1839 and 1901 were in most respects more similar to each
other in practice and sentiment than either is to any year in the
present or recent past. If it is hard to trace aggregate homicide
rates across the span of the late nineteenth century, it is even
more difficult to compare the cumulative results with figures for
the late twentieth. Differences in medical technology and legal
practice as well as the great demographic and social changes of
the last three generations make it impossible to find truly equivalent indices of violent behavior. The significance of the issue,
however, demands the effort. At the worst it is possible to get
some perspective on the problems of aggregate comparison,
while in some specific areas better information is available. And
differences in the nature, treatment, and incidence of homicide,
along with the changing involvement of various population
subgroups, are critically important to understanding the
changes wrought by urban growth.

> The weakness of the net of criminal justice in Philadelphia
> . . . is notorious . . .
>
> ✓   Presentment of grand jury, January sessions, 1840
> quoted in *Public Ledger*, February 4, 1840

There are several sources of modern statistical information that may be used to compare roughly the situation in contemporary Philadelphia with that in the previous century. One is Marvin Wolfgang's classic study *Patterns in Criminal Homicide*, based on an analysis of all cases in that city reported for 1948 through 1952.[1] Official information provided by the Philadelphia police, health office, and Court of Common Pleas constitutes a second source for 1969 through 1971.[2] Last is a study by Frank Hartleroad, modeled on Wolfgang's and similarly based on police records, which samples the period from the middle of 1972 through the end of 1974.[3] None of these is fully comparable either with the others or with the figures for the previous century. This chapter discusses the reasons for this lack of comparability. But the most nearly comparable information, the number of persons officially accused of some degree of criminal homicide, is at least a starting point. These figures are shown in Table 14.

Because of the methods of enumeration—indictments for the earlier period and arrests for the latter two—the difference between the nineteenth and the twentieth centuries is considerably overstated, but the official increase is great nonetheless.[4] More difficult to determine is how much of the increase is "real" and how much of it merely statistical; harder yet is the problem of what the figures mean in terms of aggressive, assaultive, or reckless behavior.

Two of the most important factors affecting the real rates have tended to pull them in opposite directions. One of these is the enormous advance made in medicine, especially in the treatment of traumatic injuries; the other is the continued growth of a weapons, particularly guns, culture. Some raw material for an evaluation of both developments is shown in Table 15, which compares the means used in committing homicides during the three periods and, as a related index, the amount of time elapsed

Table 14. Number and rate per 100,000 population of persons officially accused of nonaccidental criminal homicide in 3 periods.

Years	Number	Incidence
1839-1901	1,359	3.0
1948-1952	537	4.2
1969-1971	1,499	25.7

Source: See appendix B and chapter 5, note 4.

between the act and death. The table, like all of those involving comparison across time, is badly flawed by differences in the available information.[5] But however rough the figures, two basic conclusions stand out strongly.

First, a considerable number of the nineteenth-century victims would not have died in the two more recent periods. In either 1950 or 1970 a phone call could summon an emergency team equipped with whole blood and a motor-driven ambulance to take the injured party to a specialized treatment center. In the previous century the modal procedure was to fetch a doc-

Table 15. Weapon used and time of victim's death, by percent, in all
criminal homicides, in 3 periods.[1]

	1839-1901	1948-1952	1972-1974
Weapon			
Firearms	25	33	56
Sharp instrument	25	36	31
Blunt instrument	17	9	3
Fists, feet, body	21	16	5
Other	12	6	5
Time of death			
Within 24 hours	67	78	89
After 24 hours	33	22	11

Source: See chapter 5, notes 3 and 5, and appendix B; Wolfgang, *Homicide*, pp. 85, 115.
1. Totals for 1839-1901 are for cases coming to trial only.

tor, often on foot; neither blood transfusions nor most other emergency procedures were available anywhere, and a trip to the hospital, by carriage or wagon, was reserved for cases that required major and, by definition, nonemergency surgery, or perhaps continual nursing care.

A complicating factor, however, is the larger proportion of nineteenth-century homicides involving weapons not normally considered lethal—sticks and stones, fists and feet. Between one-third and one-half of the victims in cases tried between 1839 and 1901 were killed without the aid of either guns or sharp instruments; the proportion would doubtless be greater if the figures included those who were indicted but not tried, since the use of a deadly weapon tended to increase the chances for successful prosecution. And modern medicine has made far greater advances in treating sharp, relatively clean wounds than it has in repairing the multiple injuries characteristic of nineteenth-century stompings and beatings.

The differing patterns of weapons used also suggests the other and opposite way in which changing technology has affected the homicide rate. It is not usual and was never easy for an adult human being to beat, choke, or even bludgeon another to death. Given the degree of ferocity indicated by the number of times this feat was performed between 1839 and 1901, it seems clear that the murder rate would have been sharply higher had weapons been as available as in 1950 or certainly 1970.

However these offsetting factors are weighed, the most important condition affecting comparison of the incidence of homicide involves not the "real" but the reported rates, because of differences in the two systems of criminal justice at every level.

The treatment of homicide cases in Philadelphia was a matter of serious professional concern in 1950 and, despite the strain of overload, in 1970. Although modern police rarely need and still more rarely use all the expertise available to them, by comparison with their counterparts in the previous century they have an enormous battery of technological resources available for any given case. More important than the way is the will; a contemporary homicide division is at or near the top of the hierarchy of prestige within the department, representing for many officers the culmination of their career ambition. By statistical measure this pride is justifiable. Marvin Wolfgang's definition of a "solved" homicide is one in which, after a coroner or equivalent official has declared that a criminal killing has occurred, the police are able to identify a suspect and ideally to arrest one.[6] Of 588 homicides reported during 1948-1952, 558 or nearly 94 percent were solved in this way, and all but 13 suspects were arrested.[7] This average, 91.3 percent "cleared by arrest," or at least warrant, was very close to that reported for other cities in the same period, and close also to that reported for the same department a generation later. During 1969-1971, of 1,058 homicides reported, some 946 or 89.4 percent were similarly cleared.[8]

At the same time and by comparable standards, the office of district attorney was operating with parallel efficiency. Precisely two-thirds of those charged, some 66.7 percent, were convicted of criminal homicide during 1948-1952; 20.1 percent were acquitted in court, 3.5 percent were nol-prossed, and the remainder still awaited trial, or had died, been declared insane, or otherwise failed to complete the course.[9] The closest parallel figures for 1969-1971 are: 69.6 percent of those charged with criminal homicide convicted, 24.7 percent acquitted, while the rest suffered or enjoyed a variety of fates less legally decisive.[10]

Although there is no equivalent means of measuring the coroner's performance in the first stage of the homicide processing system, it seems that during the late 1940s and early 1950s that office was run on a largely professional basis, with a corps of trained pathologists working under the elected head. In 1953 the office of coroner was abolished as an unnecessary anachronism, and the city turned instead to an appointed medical examiner to run the wholly professional operation that has existed ever since.[11]

The strong contrast between this situation and conditions in the nineteenth century begins with the record for homicide convictions. The growing assertiveness and effectiveness of the district attorney was described in chapter 4, but his rate of success never approached that of his modern counterparts. Even by the end of the century, in 1895-1901, when the threshold of tolerance of violence reached its lowest point, the odds were against conviction for any death-related crime except for the one type unique to the period; four of the six prosecutions for attempted suicide were concluded successfully, sending one man to an insane asylum while the others suffered costs, fines, and suspended sentences.

The low rate of conviction for homicide was partly caused by problems of detection or of obtaining evidence, which weakened many cases. But even more important, these problems, some of them inherent in the nature of nineteenth-century homicides, others in the limitations of the police and detective systems, prevented many other cases from getting fed into the machinery of criminal justice at all.

The patterns evident among those homicide cases that came to trial must have been even clearer among those cases that did not; many were of a kind that makes detection difficult even now. The modern rate of "clearance" results not from sophisticated technology or detective work but from the fact that most killings present few problems to an experienced officer. The presence of a gun, often traceable, makes it hard to deny felonious intent, and the killer, often a friend or relative of the victim and found within the same four walls, usually makes little effort to do so. Wolfgang identified seven conditions that tend to differentiate "unsolved" cases from those generally cleared by arrest.[12] One of these conditions, an aged victim, cannot be evaluated because of deficiencies in the nineteenth-century data. It probably overlaps a second, robbery as apparent motive, which requires separate discussion, as does the matter of day of the week. Every other type of "difficult" case was more characteristic of the previous century than of this one. While one of them— white victim—is simply the result of demographic change in Philadelphia, the others are all significant. One, killings that do not involve weapons, has been outlined above. The other two, killings that occur outside the home and killings of strangers, are shown in Table 16.[13]

City streets have always been thought dangerous at night, but relative to the total number of killings, this was more true in the nineteenth century than in the mid-twentieth, when more

Table 16.   Location of homicides, and relationship between victim and
accused, by percent, in 2 periods.[1]

	1839-1901	1948-1952
Location		
Home	31	51
Street	39	30
Saloon, bar	12	8
Other	18	12
Relationship		
Family	22	25
Acquaintance	48	61
Stranger	30	14

Source: See appendix B, and Wolfgang, *Homicide*, pp. 123, 207.
1. Totals for 1839-1901 are for cases coming to trial only.

murders occurred in the home than in all other places combined. The differing pattern seems to result from two tangentially related circumstances. One is that the kinds of people
most likely to commit homicides, overwhelmingly poor and
lower class, were perhaps less likely in the nineteenth century to
be found at home at all. Philadelphia was always proud of its
reputation as "the City of Homes," and housing conditions between 1839 and 1901 were generally less miserable than those in
other metropolitan areas. But a large number of people lived in
shacks or airless cellars. Even married couples often rented single rooms, and for transient bachelors, who were one of the
most violence-prone groups in the population, life in boarding-
houses was the rule. Even the houses of the respectable working
class offered few amenities and fewer diversions. The rate of literacy was not high by later standards, and in the absence of ra-
dio, television, and even central heating, many men must have
sought out the saloon for the simple comforts as well as the
other forms of solace that it offered. The time spent in transit
could be even more exciting or hazardous, with the streets full
of animals, activity, and people, all in open contact, none enclosed in moving metal shells. At the same time, evenings spent

at home were, if not necessarily quiet, at least less dangerous than family occasions a century later.[14] Without handguns stashed nearby, domestic arguments were less likely to erupt into truly lethal violence.

Whatever the reasons behind their changing incidence, killings in the streets or by strangers pose obvious problems of solution. So does the one glaring anomaly in Wolfgang's categories of unsolved cases; robbery as a motive for murder, unlike most of the others, was proportionately more common in the midtwentieth century, among those cases available for analysis, than in the nineteenth. The figures are 8.1 percent and 2.8 percent, respectively. But it is hard to believe that the latter figure is an accurate representation of reality, given the opportunities offered by drunken roisterers, frequent collisions between strangers, the apparent violence of street life generally. It appears that many robbery-murders were simply not indicted, for several reasons. The typical robbery involves at least a minimum of calculation, always an attempt to flee, and usually a determination to deny all guilt. Moreover, in the nineteenth century, most were committed by young men without extensive criminal connections. In the major eastern cities the fraternity of professional thieves had originated in the British underworld, one which traditionally built upon careful skills and stealth rather than violence. The detective system was in turn not only a response to but in origin often an outgrowth of this underworld.[15] Its apparent failure to deal satisfactorily with robbery-murder simply underlines the fact that it was not adapted to dealing with the homicidal violence of amateurs generally.

Before the establishment of professional police, detective work, whether by peace officers or private citizens, was usually done for a fee, reward, or percentage. Even afterward, well into the 1850s and 1860s, detectives on the public payroll were almost wholly concerned with professionals or semiprofessionals, men and women with whom they enjoyed a kind of symbiotic relationship and from whose ranks they were often drawn. Philadelphia's first police detectives were detailed in 1859, and in their earliest years made much the same kinds of arrests as the force in general.[16] Later they specialized in crimes against property, suffering through the reorganizations and scandals common to contemporary police and inevitable in a working environment so full of opportunities for corruption. If anything distinguished them from their counterparts in other eastern cities it was that there were so few of them; as late as 1898 there were only fifteen detectives for the entire city.[17]

Although they were sometimes called upon to work in homicide cases, nothing in the backgrounds of these men prepared them to do it well. None specialized in the investigation of murder, and although experienced in finding known rogues, they had no devices, apart from a certain cynical expertise in questioning suspects, for identifying unknown killers. In some cases solving a homicide might bring inner rewards, but few offered anything more tangible, and detectives cannot have relished such assignments. Their record reflects the situation.

The hundreds of murder indictments collected for this study include incidents of almost every description, some notorious, some highly unusual. Herman Webster Mudgett, alias Dr. H. H. Holmes, perhaps the most celebrated mass murderer of the century, was caught in 1895—by a private insurance agent—and hanged for a single killing in Philadelphia.[18] The series prepared for this study includes two matricides, two others in which mothers killed adult sons, one in which a young woman was murdered by her grandfather. But the most strikingly unique episode was the murder of six-year-old Mary Mohrman on September 6, 1868.[19]

Mary was found dead on an open lot near Sixth and Susquehanna, victim of a sexual attack and strangulation. Under pressure of public indignation, the police arrested some thirteen men over the next few weeks before abandoning active interest in the case. A year later, however, a young married man named Charles Hanlon, a neighbor of the Mohrman family, attempted to assault a woman with a brick and was arrested by her escort. Just a month after that case was dismissed, in November 1869, Hanlon was again arrested for assaulting a female, this time a ten-year-old girl, and was sentenced, under the name of Charles E. Harris, to five years in Moyamensing Prison. The local alderman, however, managed to make the connection between Hanlon and Harris, and arranged to bring in two city detectives, who planted themselves in the prison and amid much hugger-mugger arranged the suspect's "confession" to a cellmate. Hanlon immediately repudiated this and produced a large number of unshakable witnesses in his own defense. The circumstances alleged by the prosecution did sound improbable in several respects, and the jury took an unusually lengthy two days to arrive at a verdict of guilty. In any case, following failure of an appeal, the young man was hanged.

What is unique about the incident is that in the sixty-three years, it is the only reported sexual assault on a murder victim of any age or sex. Such crimes are never common, but nothing that we know about the sexual habits and attitudes of Victorian Philadelphia suggests that so clean a record should be mistaken for reality. The lack cannot be explained in terms of reportage; while the *Ledger* was often reticent about details, it was not reluctant to report cases of "outrage" or "indecency," and the ritual disclaimer that certain matters were "unfit for publication" left little doubt as to what was involved. The most likely explanation for the almost total absence in the series of indictments for such crimes is that they were not solved. A secretive killer, no matter how disturbed, could easily prove cunning enough to frustrate the nineteenth-century detective system.

Weaknesses in the systems of detection and prosecution contributed to the fact that the proportion of nineteenth-century cases that were "lost" between a coroner's verdict and indictment—and thus not counted in Table 14—was far higher than the 10 percent or so that are lost between arrest and verdict in the later twentieth century. In the six years for which full coroner's verdicts are available, 1854-1857 and 1878-1880, there were 101 indictments for murder and manslaughter. But not counting infanticides, deaths from abortion, and either "excusable" or "justifiable" killings, homicide verdicts were found in 33 additional incidents. Of these, 22 were killings committed by "a person or persons unknown" and never subsequently cleared, and 11 involved a culprit named at the inquest but never indicted. Were they included, they would doubtless increase the proportion in Table 16 of street crimes and killings by strangers.

Far more important than this loss, however, was the loss at the very first level, for problems elsewhere in the system point to the need to examine the real office of the county coroner. Historically his original function, and still his most publicized, was to identify cases of homicide for reference to the prosecuting authorities. But the fee system was rigged in such a way as to make homicide cases less rewarding than either suicides or accidents, even apart from the important fact that they were ordinarily more time-consuming. And since the rest of the machinery of justice was clearly not equipped to follow through on incidents in which the slayer was not identified and at hand, in terms of social function many homicide verdicts were at best useless and at worst embarrassing, even frightening. Those that did not ultimately result in conviction implied the failure of police or prosecutors, with whom the coroner had to work. Beyond that there was little utility in probing the fates of the often marginal people, sometimes strangers to the community, whom he encountered in death. It was possible to take an active role in the office, as did Michael Dugan, clearly influenced by the exploits of his mentor, Samuel Ashbridge, who had used seventeen years as coroner as a springboard to the mayoralty.[20] But Dugan's activism, well illustrated by his handling of several cases described in chapter 4, was not medical or forensic but moral. Much like his contemporaries in the office of district attorney, he was energetic only in fixing blame upon people who had clearly been the agents of death, often accidentally, rather than in seeking out agents unknown. No society wants to be officially reminded of problems its machinery is incapable of handling. And it seems useful to explore the notion that the real function of the coroner was not merely to "label" homicides but in awkward cases to mislabel them, to filter out the hopeless or difficult ones.

One means of filtering out problems was to label killings either "excusable" or "justifiable." In 1948-1952 this was a function of the inquest, and in 1972-1974, of the district attorney in consultation with the medical examiner.[21] The legal situation in the previous century was not so clear. While the term was not used explicitly, a finding of "accidental shooting" was the functional equivalent of an "excusable" verdict. Late in the century prosecutors, as noted in chapter 4, tended to prosecute apparent accident as manslaughter, with or without the cooperation of coroners. But a considerable number of shootings still escaped the most accusing eyes, and the period around the Fourth of July, in particular, was a kind of festival of death for patriotic young men and boys.[22]

"Justifiable" homicide was, and is, a more controversial matter. All of the fourteen justifiable cases of 1948-1952 and the fully thirty-three found by Hartleroad during 1972-1974 involved killings by police officers.[23] In the nineteenth-century city the use of deadly force was generally subject to more careful scrutiny. While some cases did not result in indictment, between 1839 and 1901 nineteen peace officers were tried for homicide, a proceeding virtually unknown in late twentieth-century Philadelphia and rare anywhere in the United States. Inquest juries, however, were eager sometimes to report that a given act had been fully justified in their eyes, usually as an act of self-defense. Their legal right to do this was not established, and in one highly charged case in 1870, when an election official shot down a member of a mob that had invaded his office, the district attorney refused to honor such a verdict.[24] The function of an inquest, he insisted, was merely to determine the medical, not the legal, cause of death. The point in any case was usually moot; given the odds that prevailed under ordinary circumstances, an inquest verdict such as "death from a wound in the heart from a pistol in the hands of Robert Doran in defense of his own life, while being pursued and attacked by the deceased and others to the jury unknown"[25] was fatal to the prosecution. Five such verdicts were rendered in the six years for which records are available.

Much more important than the "justifiable" or "accidental" labels are those that are missing entirely; in every year examined there is massive evidence of accident or, more rarely, suicide verdicts rendered in dubious circumstances. Some of this may be explicable in terms of a natural reluctance to do postmortems, a problem once cited by the health office.[26] This may account in part for the notable lack of curiosity with which the coroner regarded that large number of persons "found drowned" in the rivers. But generally the failure to find homicide resulted from a more conscious kind of resistance. Coroners often took pains to quiet rumors of foul play reported in the *Ledger*, and sometimes inquest juries did so explicitly; the normally laconic docket book for 1857 contains three notations, in deaths found respectively from "intemperance," "brain fever," and "perforation of the intestines," that the case was "supposed to have been a homicide."[27]

While it is impossible to evaluate them *ex post facto*, many of these dubious findings seem egregious. Thus in May 1900 a stranger was "found drowned" in the Delaware, his pockets containing papers but no cash. Two policemen found him with his hands tied behind his back; a hotel clerk, the last to see him alive, pointed out that his bag as well as his money was missing. The verdict was, however, suicide.[28] Just three weeks later, despite Valentine Weber's insistence in his last semilucid moments that he had been assaulted and robbed outside a saloon, an inquest found that he had fractured his skull on the sidewalk.[29] The coroner was especially, and understandably, reluctant to deal with killings involving unidentified persons, as either victims or perpetrators. Virtually all verdicts pointing to a "person or persons unknown to this jury" were applied in cases in which the fact of homicide was undeniably established, as by gunshot wounds or witnesses to a street fight. In the absence of such witnesses, persons such as Weber, found outdoors with broken heads, were labeled victims of a "fall while in a state of intoxication."

The contemporary press is the only source for information about incidents that may have been mislabeled, and it is not a good one. In the earliest years, lacking an active corps of reporters, the *Public Ledger* had to rely mostly upon the coroner himself for news of violent deaths, and even by the end of the century the business of getting information was not fully independent. But despite this problem it is at least possible to establish some order of magnitude. For the five years 1839-1841, 1870, and 1900 combined, a total of eighty-two incidents resulted in indictments for homicide. For the same five years, not

counting murder-suicides, infanticides, unwitnessed "skull fractures," and routine cases in which bodies were "found drowned,"
there were fully ninety-two other deaths about which the question of foul play was raised in the pages of the conservative *Ledger*.[30]

Table 14, then, in understating the level of homicide in the
nineteenth as compared to the twentieth century, is not merely
misleading but perhaps radically so. While the "dark figure" is
by definition unknowable for any era, the evidence concerning
official weakness and even cover-up suggests that it was far
greater then than now.

> I had no idea of anything ailing my daughter as she had
> been regular every month. On Thursday she complained of
> cramps and I gave her some liquor . . . [Next morning] I
> saw the black petticoat all pinned up and lying in the cra-
> dle. I took it up and it was heavy. I said What is this? Is it a
> child? I said when did you have it? She said this morning. I
> asked her if it was dead when borne she said yes. I did not
> open the bundle . . .
>
> Testimony of Mary Ann Shuster,
> *Commonwealth V. Elizabeth Shuster,*
> *Coroner's Evidence Book,* August 5, 1875

One kind of homicide caused such especially
tangled problems for the system of criminal justice in the nineteenth century that it was rarely labeled at the inquest level and
requires a separate explanation. For the individuals involved,
the problem of unwanted pregnancy was often desperately
acute in Victorian Philadelphia. Criminal penalties were attached, or became attached, to several of the traditional strat-
egies for avoiding motherhood, and social stigma to the rest.
The established response to this cruel dilemma was to ignore its
results whenever possible and, in particular, to invoke the official sanctions as rarely and quietly as possible.

It is hard to judge the impact of Pennsylvania's P.L. 40,
which was passed in March 1870 to prevent the sale, advertise-
ment, or even description of "any drug, instrument, or appara-
tus for the purpose of preventing conception."[31] At that time a

variety of reasonably effective birth-control techniques was to some extent available, at least to middle- and upper-class Americans, and they continued in use despite a growing legal and moral campaign that may have prevented a wider clientele from using them.[32] It is somewhat easier to assess the impact of and reaction to abortion in the same period, because of a perceptive recent study by James Mohr. Mohr's book, which is concerned with both abortion and the legal-medical attack upon it in the middle and later nineteenth century, helps set the background for the information here from Philadelphia's justice system.[33]

In 1839, the year when Dr. Chauncey was tried for the fatal abortion attempt in the case of Eliza Sowers, killing a woman in the course of such an operation was in Pennsylvania considered murder in the second degree.[34] Little attention was paid to the fate of the unborn child, an attitude reinforced by the old common-law doctrine that abortion itself was not criminal until after the fetus had "quickened," usually in the sixth month. Neither contemporary medical opinion nor professional ethics presented any firm bar to those who sought to end pregnancies. And given the familiar pressures felt by the middle and upper classes in a modernizing society, there was beginning about 1840 a sharp increase in the numbers of those seeking abortion, especially among respectable married women.[35] By the middle of the 1860s, some contemporary physicians estimated that perhaps 20 or 25 percent of all conceptions were ended artificially.[36]

By that time, however, the business was under increasing attack by the more established members of the medical profession, who were concerned for a variety of reasons about the methods and qualifications of many abortionists. Armed with newly developed scientific as well as moral arguments about the sanctity of life before "quickening," these doctors joined in a crusade that benefited from generally stricter attitudes toward sexuality. Beginning in the late 1850s and continuing more strongly thereafter, these groups succeeded in persuading many states to tighten antiabortion legislation and in making the practice less acceptable everywhere.[37]

The first Philadelphia prosecution for a "simple" abortion—inducement of miscarriage only—occurred in 1857, just as the

opposition was beginning to rally. The defendant was acquitted. But two more cases resulting in death to the women involved were prosecuted successfully as murder in 1859. And in
1860 the commissioners who were appointed to revise the penal
code reported their conclusions about this as well as other problems in criminal prosecution. In line with their general strategy,
what they recommended for abortion, as for manslaughter, was
easing the penalty and widening the discretion of the court in
order to increase the rate of conviction. The first section of the
new law thus made the killing of a pregnant woman punishable
by a maximum fine of five hundred dollars and/or a maximum
sentence of seven years at labor. At the same time the commissioners broadened the definition of criminal behavior by creating a substantively new offense; according to the same statute,
any attempt at procuring a miscarriage at any stage of gesta-
tion, was an act that could be punished by up to three years in
prison.[38]

Meanwhile, during the midcentury years when the practice of
abortion apparently reached its peak, the coroner and the health
office in effect conspired to veil their awareness of the inevitable
casualties. Some of the abortifacients of the period were danger-
ously noxious liquids taken by mouth; others were injected directly into the vagina. These chemical methods were supplemented by a variety of suction devices, electric machines, and
uterine probes, most administered in utter ignorance of the
problems of contamination and sepsis.[39] Inquest juries did report that deaths were caused by bungled abortions or criminal
malpractice. But usually in these cases the notation "tetanus" or
"peritonitis," only sometimes with the key word "violence,"
was all that appeared in the *Annual Register of Deaths*.[40] It was
not until late in the century, after its actual incidence had greatly declined, that six or eight cases of abortion regularly led the
annual health office's alphabetical list of causes of death in the
city.

Prosecution for abortion of both kinds followed the same sort
of curve—a classic pattern for nineteenth-century criminal statistics—moving up as the incidence of the proscribed behavior
moved down. After the single acquittal in 1857 and the two

murder trials in the same decade, there were no indictments at all for abortion until 1869, and then an average of one a year through 1873. Between 1874 and 1880, however, there were twenty-nine; between 1881 and 1887, thirty-eight; between 1888 and 1894, thirty-six; and from 1895 through 1901, thirty-nine more.

The circumstances behind most of these cases, and sometimes even their existence, were hidden from the respectable reading public. In strong contrast to the unsensational but frank coverage given the death of Eliza Sowers in 1839, when the medical testimony was reprinted in full, the *Public Ledger* utterly ignored the first "simple" abortion case of 1857, and much of the evidence in the murder trials of 1859 was declared "unfit for publication." Thereafter a rule of reticence was generally observed, with only an occasional case earning more than a few lines in the section on the disposition of cases in the Court of Quarter Sessions. Although neither the form of the indictments nor the reportage makes it fully clear, apparently relatively few of these cases involved adult deaths. The slender evidence suggests that most indictments were formally initiated through warrants sworn by the women clients, perhaps urged on by members of the respectable medical fraternity called in to repair some damage.[41] (One indictment was discharged, according to a note in the docket unique in both form and content, "because defendant and prosecutrix have married."[42]) Those cases that were carried to verdict proved difficult to convict. Dying declarations were allowed in a few cases, and eight people were sentenced to the maximum of seven years. But abortion resulting in the death of a woman shared with "victimless" crimes the fact that most potential witnesses were deeply implicated, deeply ashamed, or both. In the others, clearly considered less serious by petit juries, the woman herself was a suspect witness. A total of 127 of the 151 persons indicted during the entire period was brought to verdict; 22 pleaded guilty and 25 were convicted, a combined rate of 31 percent of those indicted.

Whatever the effect of this somewhat ambiguous record of prosecution—it is noteworthy that after the 1860 legislation a full nine years elapsed before it was put to the test—the incidence of abortion, according to Mohr, began to decline some time during the 1870s.[43] As a result of the campaign led by the medically orthodox, certainly, fewer respectable physicians and fewer respectable women engaged in the practice. The impact of this decline on the rate of illegitimacy is less easy to gauge, since it is unclear how many single women of the poorer classes sought abortions at any time. Mohr has found greatly differing prices quoted, but even in the relatively unharried 1860s, reliable operations cost a minimum of one hundred dollars and much more if the traffic would bear it.[44] As a practical solution to the problem of unwanted pregnancy, that sum was far beyond the reach of most women, particularly the unmarried. While prostitutes presumably had the information and the contacts to assure themselves of reasonably effective service at appropriate rates, most women did not.

Both before and after the antiabortion campaign large numbers of reluctant women carried their pregnancies to term. And at that point, if the baby was illegitimate and still unwanted, the available choices were all distasteful or worse. The law in Philadelphia allowed only two courses: a woman might bring an action for "fornication and bastardy" or surrender her child to the Guardians of the Poor.

An action for bastardy was in form a criminal complaint, triable in the Court of Quarter Sessions, but in substance it was a civil suit against the alleged father of the child, usually brought before the birth. A significant number of these were filed each year, twenty or so in the 1840s, over a hundred by the 1890s.[45] Much like assault warrants, they collectively represent the substitution of official processes for private justice. Perhaps the threat of court action was enough to win some sort of settlement for an unwed mother. But if carried out in full, the impersonal mechanism of the law must have seemed to many girls a poor substitute for an angry visit from father or brothers. It is difficult to interpret the outcomes of many cases, owing to the large proportion of indictments that were ignored, nol-prossed, or otherwise lost in the legal process. In 1870, of thirty-one indictments, ten resulted in conviction, nine in acquittals before a jury, and the other twelve were not brought to verdict; they were either settled or not thought strong enough for trial. The situation was similar in both 1839 and 1901; so was the typical "sentence," a flat fee for lying-in expenses and a weekly charge for child support, varying slightly with the case. The size of these awards did change somewhat; in 1839, $10 for birthing expenses and 62½¢ weekly support payments were most typical; in 1870 and 1900, the fees were $25 to $35 and $1.25 to $2.00. Payment was only occasionally guaranteed by a bond administered by the Guardians of the Poor.

Perhaps even with such an award, and certainly without one, a mother might consider the Guardians directly. If done openly, this course involved not only interrogation and certain shame immediately but possible liability later; if the woman's financial situation improved, through marriage or otherwise, she could be assessed for supporting the child.[46] Even if approached anonymously, through a basket left at the gate, the Blockley Almshouse was justly regarded with horror; even its directors conceded that it was not equipped to keep babies, certainly not newborns, alive for long.[47]

The most palatable alternative was to find a substitute parent or parents. Neighborhood women occasionally adopted foundlings quite spontaneously. An even better device was reported in the *Ledger* in September 1840, when an infant was specifically ticketed with a young man's name and address: "The Benedict, for he is one, immediately procured a wet nurse, and has complied thus far with the request."[48] Kindly strangers in a railway terminal could be asked to watch a child while the mother went to the toilet and failed to return; this was abandonment, a criminal offense, for which arrests, but virtually no prosecutions, were made every year.[49] (On one occasion a young woman accused of abandoning a child produced a newborn before the magistrate and was asked, in quasi-Solomonic fashion, to nurse it as proof of her maternity; she did.[50]) Happy endings were, however, rare. The usual fate of children left untended was to be handed over to the watch or police and through them to the Guardians and the almshouse.

Among those with money to spend, it was common to hire a "nurse" to preside over the baby's almost inevitable decline and death. In August 1840 a woman from Bucks County traveled into the city in search of such a nurse, who then simply turned the infant over to a "colored man" for disposal.[51] In 1870 a house for illegitimate children reportedly provided a diet of loaf sugar and watered cow's milk for three dollars a week—twice the cost of bastardy support payments—during the four to five months that the infants usually survived.[52] By 1900 strict licensing laws had made such "baby farms" illegal but not unknown, and dead infants were still dumped in suspicious numbers on certain empty lots.[53]

Given these alternatives, which provided infanticide with at least some thin cover for conscience's sake, the open and willful killing of a newborn child must have been an act of extreme desperation. It is strictly impossible to infer the typical circumstances from the few cases that came to trial. But if abortion or a bastardy suit required friends or contacts, abandonment a certain boldness, and a nurse some substantial sum of money, murder was surely reserved for the most destitute and frightened of mothers. Virtually all of those indicted were not only unwed but apparently alone. Under the circumstances usual to these indictments, the fact of murder would have been impossible to hide from any confidante, and the exceptional male accused as accessory betrays the rule.[54]

The fact that successful prosecution in these cases was extremely difficult was recognized in a series of retreats from that seventeenth-century English law that had first declared it a capital crime to "conceal the death of a bastard child."[55] The penalty, as for murder, was hanging, the main difference being that the burden of proof, uniquely, lay with the accused; the act of concealment was presumptive evidence of infanticide unless a witness could confirm the mother's testimony that the baby had been stillborn. In the Pennsylvania penal code of 1794, which in its time was a model of humaneness, the presumption of live birth was eliminated. The revised code of 1860 went still further by making concealment a separate and substantive offense whether the child was born alive or dead, carrying a maximum of three years at hard labor. This allowed not only for a united indictment for murder and concealment, which had been the usual procedure, but for either charge—usually concealment—alone. And in significant contrast to the trend in other cases, the practice toward century's end was to omit the murder charge entirely and try for an almost symbolic conviction for concealment, often obtained through a bargained plea of guilty and resulting in a light or suspended sentence.

The circumstance that forced this long and, for the prosecution, uncharacteristic retreat was the moral impossibility of dealing with the biological problem that had originally inspired 21 Jac. I, ch. 27, back in 1607. It was as simple quietly to kill an infant in nineteenth-century Philadelphia as it had been in seventeenth-century London. Dozens of newborns were "overlaid" each year, allegedly suffocated by mothers who rolled on top of them while asleep or drunk. Hundreds more died of "inanition" and other ailments defined with equal precision. Most important, when a birth was unattended, as happened often among the unwed, the line between a natural and an artificial death was virtually impossible to detect.[56] The law of 1860 could do nothing to ease the problem of detection, and while legislators could manipulate such abstractions as the balance of proof, prosecutors could not so manipulate the balance of sympathy.

It is hard to learn much about cases of concealment or infanticide. The *Public Ledger* during the 1840s reported many cases as news when they happened and titillated its readers uncharacteristically with the notion that "this is a most interesting case," or even that "some of its features strongly resemble Scott's tale of the Heart of Midlothian."[57] But the reader was expected to satisfy his or her curiosity in the courtroom, for the paper reported only the barest information about trials, usually name, date, and verdict only. Later in the century the *Ledger* stopped reporting such incidents as current news, confining itself to brief trial notices that appeared only some weeks or months after the event. By 1900 the last case in the series, in which concealment alone was charged, did not even make the daily summary of "Court Intelligence."[58]

Still there is information enough to suggest the problems faced by the district attorney. Some fifty-nine cases came to verdict between 1839 and 1901, fairly well distributed through the decades. But since any woman who took the most elementary precautions would never have to answer for such a crime, it was obvious to all that only a fraction of the guilty were ever brought to the bar. More desperate than most who had to labor through unwanted pregnancies, the ones indicted were often emotionally disturbed as well, to the point of utter recklessness. The child was usually strangled within moments of birth, and the typical means of disposal in the incidents brought to trial was to throw it into the privy, often shared by five or six families and sometimes the site of the unattended birth itself. Even this rudimentary attempt to escape detection was sometimes overlooked, and the child was thrown from a window or simply left mutilated in a bedroom or attic. Under such circumstances there was rarely a question of what had happened, why, or by whom. But of the fifty-nine cases that reached the courtroom— not counting those ignored, nol-prossed, or otherwise aborted short of trial—only one resulted in a first-degree murder verdict and three in convictions for murder in the second degree. Five were convicted of voluntary and three of involuntary manslaughter, four of "concealment of the death of bastard child"; fully forty-two were declared not guilty, four of them by reason of insanity. The sole death sentence was pronounced over Hester Vaughn, who waited some time after the child's birth in February 1868 before bludgeoning it to death.[59] Several of the six men indicted were included in the convictions; many of the convicted women were given suspended sentences or immediate pardons. In the case that heads this section the Shuster infant was found with its throat torn and crushed, right next to the bed it was born in; its mother was acquitted. Petit jurors, clearly, had little stomach for inflicting further punishment.

If in dealing with adult homicides the purpose of the coroner's inquest was to filter out cases that the system was unable to handle in any socially useful fashion, this function was even more evident in the case of infant deaths. Official Philadelphia never abandoned its "anxiety," as the penal code commissioners put it, "for the protection of human life."[60] But it had no effec-

tive means of curbing the rate of infanticide. Inquest juries identified small victims when they had to, sometimes overstepping
their bounds in suggesting, for example, that a child had died of
"a fall from a window thrown by its mother while temporarily
insane."[61] It was better to find "inhalation of gasses on being accidentally dropped in a well," best to find nothing questionable
at all.[62] The coroner was called when a baby died without an at-
tending physician, or more rarely when a doctor refused to sign
a death certificate. But he had neither the desire nor the resources to label these incidents suspicious.

Accordingly there is only one possible index to the magnitude
of nineteenth-century infanticide, and that is applicable only to
a particular subcategory, the number of "unknown" infants listed annually in the death register.[63] These "unknown" cases were
succinctly described by coroner's clerk Michael Doran in 1879
as "newborns found in the streets and on lots etc."[64] They were
almost never listed as victims of infanticide. Coroners in the
1860s and 1870s usually matched the cause of death to the condition, writing "unknown" in both spaces on the death certificates. Late-century physicians were less ready to admit their ignorance and more inclined to suggest "asphyxia" or "exposure"
or sometimes "stillborn." Few postmortems were held; there
was little point. It is impossible to state precisely how many of
these small bodies represented true infanticides; all that can be
said is that someone badly wanted to get rid of them while remaining anonymous themselves. A few were indeed stillborn;
on the evidence for those years (by no means all) when that condition was specifically noted, they amounted to perhaps 5 percent of the total. Some died of natural causes and were thrown
out by the mother or others in attendance to spare the minimal
trouble of burial at city expense—itself an appalling index of
wretchedness. But considered simply as the one pool that most
obviously contains a large number of unlabeled infanticides,
this "unknown" category was a large one. In the modern city,
two or three infants a year are found dead in the open, each of
them headline news.[65] Between 1861 and 1901 the annual aver-

age was more than fifty-five. Like homicide itself, the incidence was dropping with time: 12.3 of these "found dead" cases per 100,000 were averaged in the 1860s, 5.0 in the 1890s.

> The mass of petty depradations upon property in our vicinity within the last few years has been perpetrated by Germans recently arrived . . .
>
> The Irish, their poverty considered, are seldom accused of larcenies, etc. When they do steal they are generally in liquor. Assaults and batteries and other offenses arising from hot blood are the charges generally alleged against Irishmen . . .
>
> The number of colored persons in our prisons is, when the extent of that population is compared with the other, fearfully great . . . [but] their various social disadvantages are so great, that we need not marvel.
>
> Three statements from the *Public Ledger*, November 5, 1839

Not only the rates but also the patterns of homicide in complex societies vary enormously among groups. In terms of significant difference, three of the most important groups in nineteenth-century Philadelphia were women, immigrants, and blacks. The changing patterns of their behavior may be of some interest in itself; more importantly for this study, they provide information essential to an explanation of the long-term trend in the population as a whole.

The problem of infanticide creates a special paradox with respect to differences between the sexes. Men in virtually all societies are credited with far more homicides than women. But if it were possible to find the "real," as distinct from the officially recorded, number of killings in Philadelphia in the previous century and to include infanticides in that number, the figures would perhaps reveal that women committed murder at a higher rate than any other identifiable subgroup in the population.

Omitting the uncounted infanticides, however, as quantitatively incalculable and qualitatively different from most other homicides, the murder rate for nineteenth-century women was very low. During the whole period 1839-1901, 9.8 percent of all accused were female, which is little more than half the 17.6 percent found in 1948-1952 and two-thirds of the 13.2 percent in 1972-1974.[66] If the known infanticides are omitted, the disproportion is much greater. Of the 124 women counted in the nineteenth-century series, 53 were accused of this crime, which, at least on the record, was much rarer by 1950 and virtually unknown in the 1970s.[67] The significance of pregnancy among the unmarried has been transformed entirely, because of a rise in the level of living, changes in the moral climate, and the proliferation of social agencies and alternatives of several kinds.

Two tangentially related developments, social and material, seem to account for the change in the rate of adult killings by women. One of these is the change in sex roles generally. It has been argued that the increasing involvement of women in serious crime of several kinds is a reflection of greater vigor and confidence, resulting in behavior more nearly resembling that of men.[68] Certainly the kinds of homicide committed by white women in the Victorian era reflect a severely restricted role; there was one single killing as part of a robbery; the overwhelming proportion occurred in the home and involved relatives or boarders, and virtually all of the rest also resulted from domestic or sexual problems.

The other factor that held down the rate for women follows naturally; although the figures for assault and battery indicate that domesticity could be violent, for most of the population the lack of guns, or "equalizers," meant that violence was less likely to prove fatal to husbands than to wives. By the mid-twentieth century women were almost as likely to shoot their victims to death as were men.[69] But firearms deaths in the nineteenth century were not nearly so domestic as murders in general. A little more than 31 percent of all killings were committed in the home of one or both of the parties, but less than 15 percent of the shootings. Guns, as noted earlier, did not come readily to hand in the course of argument conducted in bedrooms or kitchens.

Ethnic differences among accused killers are for purposes of this study even more significant than differences in sex, but they are neither so dramatic nor so easily explained. As a further complication, they are not so easily measured, either. One set of statistics is indirect and the other inherently flawed, in that origins can be determined only on the basis of surnames, often wretchedly spelled by indifferent reporters and clerks.

The indirect measure is provided by the official death statistics published by the health office. As noted in chapter 4, these are not an accurate guide to the "real" number of homicide victims, but there is no reason to doubt that the listed proportion of the foreign-born is a rough reflection of the real one. It may be assumed further, as in many studies, that the killers and victims collectively resembled each other in terms of ethnicity as in most other matters except for sex. Between the second half of 1860 and 1901, of 751 homicide victims listed in the health records, 57 percent were reportedly native-born, 33 percent foreign, and 9 percent unknown. If the unknowns are distributed proportionately, the percentage of immigrants was some 36 percent. Although that figure is not, perhaps, higher than might be expected in a group of generally low economic status, it is higher than the proportion of the foreign-born in the whole population, which was nearly 30 percent in 1860 and descended irregularly to 23 percent in 1900. Immigrant status in itself was not significant, however, in that most foreign-born ethnic groups in Philadelphia were apparently less inclined to violence than native Americans.

Among the so-called "new" immigrants, those who characteristically arrived late in the century and were not yet very numerous in 1901, neither the Jews nor the Eastern Europeans generally were accused of as many as ten homicides in all the years from 1839 to 1901. Only the Italians, among these late-comers, were indicted at a rate greater than their percentage in the population at large. The number of killings charged to people with Italian names is somewhat inflated by the fact that there were proportionately more young adult males among them than among natives, and by the fact that by the end of the century the threshold of tolerance had already fallen considerably— both Frank Di Genna and Antonio Marmorello, whose multiple misfortunes are described at the end of chapter 4, are included in the count. Still, the thirty-four names in the group, virtually all dating from the late 1880s, constitute a high figure. During the ten years between 1891 and 1900 the homicide rate per 100,000 of the Italian-born was 6.7, more than three times the general average.

Apart from Protestant Britishers, there were only two numerically important groups with a long history of immigration to the city. Of these the Germans are clearly underrepresented in the records. There are only fifty-four unmistakably Germanic names among those indicted, representing not only those born in Germany but also those whose families had been in this country since the middle of the eighteenth century, when émigrés from the Rhineland first began to arrive in southeastern Pennsylvania. But this low figure is more than offset by the fact that the Irish, numerically the most important of the nineteenth-century immigrants, behaved violently enough to pull up the average for all of the foreign-born.

It is perhaps more difficult to determine Irish ancestry than any other kind on the basis of characteristic surnames, which is a highly conservative method of measuring the numbers of the group.[70] Also, because of the long history of emigration from the island, it is more difficult than with any other except the Germans to distinguish the foreign-born generation from those that followed. The peak years of arrival were the middle 1840s and early 1850s, during and just after the Great Famine, and the United States Census traces a steadily declining proportion of Irish natives afterward: 17.6 percent of the population of Philadelphia in 1850, 16.9 percent in 1860, 13.9 percent in 1870, 12 percent in 1880, 10 percent in 1890, 7.6 percent in 1900. Since the number of those actually born in Ireland was constantly reinforced by natural increase, however, the leading historian of Philadelphia's Irish estimates that with these descendants included, the group averaged close to 20 percent of the population throughout those decades.[71] Those with clearly Irish names, over the whole period, accounted for a little over 23 percent of all homicide indictments; those of Irish ethnic background—counting the Lanes, Clarks, and Smiths among them—may be calculated at perhaps 30 percent, or one and one-half times the general average.[72]

Except for its higher rate of occurrence, however, homicide

among the Irish was not significantly distinctive. Irishmen and women tended to kill the same sorts of persons, in the same sorts of places, and with the same sorts of weapons as the rest of the white population. And the Irish trend was, with something of a time lag, closely parallel to the general trend. Counting only those with clearly Irish surnames, their percentage of all indicted was 24 percent during 1839-1859, 27 percent during 1860-1880, and only 17 percent during 1881-1901, indicating that a process of pacification was well under way.

The black population of Philadelphia was never so large as the Irish, but its experience with homicide was at least as significant. No major group had a higher rate of indictment, as the 147 identifiably black persons indicted between 1839 and 1901 may be computed at 7.5 per 100,000—itself an understatement—or close to three times the rate for whites.[73] What makes this rate significant is not merely that it is high, but that its direction and the patterns behind it were, unlike those for the Irish, markedly different from those of the rest of the population.

While poverty and discrimination pervaded virtually all aspects of life in black neighborhoods, the method of handling of homicide cases in the criminal justice system does not seem in itself to have been an important instrument of oppression. The rate of conviction for all identifiable blacks accused of homicide was somewhat higher, 58 percent, than the conviction rate for whites, which was 48 percent. But since the majority of indictments, as with most others, were for killings within the group, what this indicates is that unlike the situation in the South during the same period, black-on-black homicide was treated as a serious matter in Philadelphia.

A better index of discrimination in the system is the outcome of trials involving interracial killings. Black neighborhoods at that time were by modern standards neither large nor tightly defined, and for many reasons their residents continually interacted with whites. One result was a rate of interracial homicide far higher than is now usual; fully 49 of the 147 were indicted for killing white persons in a total of 35 incidents. Conversely, 37 whites were accused of killing blacks in just 26 incidents.

What is remarkable is that the proportion of blacks declared guilty in these cases was rather lower than the general average in homicide cases, and in terms of the number of separate incidents involved (a pattern not so clear with respect to number of persons), it was virtually the same as the conviction rate for whites killing blacks; see Table 17.

These figures do not mean that the atmosphere of nineteenth-century Philadelphia was even tolerably free of racism. Several of the white-black episodes were clearly motivated at least in part by racial hatred, and accounts of violence of all kinds make it clear that in many areas it was dangerous for blacks to stray abroad, especially at night. But although the streets were dangerous, the courts, in dealing with the most serious of accusations, functioned in a reasonably evenhanded and sometimes even protective fashion. Representatives of the city's elite—the management of the *Ledger*, an indignant judge, a minister who had witnessed a small race riot—were the most likely to assume an overtly protective role. But even ethnically mixed and middle-class white juries were careful to observe the forms and often to achieve the substance of a color-blind impartiality.

Sometimes the observance of form was the only real function of a trial. This was surely true in the case of Officer John F. Roan, who shot an unidentified black man to death in the course of attempting an arrest in October 1859.[74] Roan had stopped the stranger on suspicion and found him with a bag full of stolen poultry; he and the one important witness testified that there was a fight—Roan claimed the man had hit him with a stone—that ended only with the fatal shot. With an officer of the city pitted against an anonymous chicken thief, the verdict, inevitably, was not guilty. Nevertheless the indictment had been drawn, the bill approved, and the trial held.

The same insistence upon observing the forms was dramatically evident, in reverse, during the trials of Amos Stirling, Henry Ivory, and Charles Perry, three black men indicted in 1900 for the robbery and murder of Roy Wilson White. While the *Public Ledger* was careful, as was its policy, not to treat the incident in inflammatory fashion, the circumstances were inherently sensational. Given the barest clues to the crime, committed just outside the West Philadelphia railway terminal on the night of May 19, city detectives directed a rare "manhunt" through three states over a full week before catching the men accused.[75] Robbers were not often tried for murder—certainly not three at once—and their chances for acquittal were always rather slight.[76] White had been a socially prominent young man, recently awarded a degree from nearby Haverford College, and serving, at the time of his death, as a popular lecturer at the University of Pennsylvania's law school. None of the three accused, in contrast, had any real ties to the city, and Stirling, the alleged leader, had been literally passing through on the day of the killing. The state's case was strong, based on Perry's confession, and all three were convicted and hanged. But at the end of a century in which a trial for murder often occupied no more than a single morning, with a jury voting conviction in twenty minutes, in this case more than three months elapsed between the August session when the three were arraigned and November 15, when Ivory was sentenced. Six court-appointed lawyers, all volunteers, a group considerably more distinguished than the usual run of the criminal bar, took much of the time by successfully demanding separate trials, vigorously challenging jurors for prejudice, submitting a battery of motions, and altogether accounting for an unprecedented twenty-one pages in the docket book. The city's elite were clearly determined not to allow anything resembling lynch law to besmirch its reputation.

More than form was involved in the trial of William Whitesides for the murder of Henry Truman in the spring of 1870.[77] Whitesides, a policeman, was called the afternoon of April 1 to Tim Buckley's Grocery, at 709 Saint Mary's Street, when Buckley complained that a crowd of blacks was making trouble. Whitesides made an arrest, but his captive broke away and fled down an alley into an all-black neighborhood, the officer in pursuit. What happened next, according to a witness for the commonwealth, was that Truman, unaware of the business at Buckley's, saw a uniformed man run out of the alley at him, asked "What's the matter?" and was answered with a shot in the stomach. Whitesides's version was that he emerged into a hos-

tile crowd that bombarded him with cries of "Kill the white
————!" and, more pointedly, with paving stones; Truman was
merely a victim of a warning shot gone awry. Although the policeman's wife and daughter were prominently on view in the
courtroom, and the only contrary testimony was sworn by
black observers—the year before any blacks were eligible to
vote in the city—the jury chose to convict for manslaughter. It
was the only conviction for any of the nineteen policemen
brought in for "line-of-duty" killings between 1839 and 1901,
and possibly the only one in the history of the city.

As in trials, so in the other stages of criminal proceedings,
there is no clear evidence of systematic bias in the administration of homicide cases. While the reliability of the official statistics in cases involving blacks is no better than in others generally, there is no reason to doubt that the disparity between the
black and white rates of indictment is a rough index of disparity
in the rates of homicides committed. The nature and type of
these killings reflect a real difference in patterns of behavior, a
difference that helps explain why more blacks than whites were
tried for interracial murders. Table 17 indicates the pattern of
these trials by race, sex, and outcome.

The most obvious differences are those that reveal the lop-
sided interaction between the races. White killings of blacks reflect superficial contacts; the great majority of them occurred
among males, strangers or perhaps slight acquaintances encountered in the streets. The element of racial antagonism typically helped to clarify the two sides in an election riot, lowered
the flash point in an argument after a ball game, or simply
served as the spark for eruptive, stomping belligerence. The situations in which blacks of either sex killed whites were much
more various. Some of the all-male encounters represent the opposite side of the characteristic white-black affray, although
there appears to be no incident in which black hatred or resent-
ment per se played a clearly decisive role. A few of the others
occurred because blacks were more deeply involved in white society, as servants for example, than vice versa. But many indicate what W. E. B. DuBois pointed out in his classic study of
Philadelphia, that the marginal and sometimes hopelessly de-

Table 17.   Trial outcomes of interracial homicides, 1839-1901.

Accused	Victim	No. guilty	No. not guilty
Black male	White male	17	12
Black male	White female	4	3
Black female	White male	0	6
Black female	White female	3	4[1]
Total		24	25
		(18 episodes)	(17 episodes)
White male	Black male	13	20
White male	Black female	2	1
White female	Black male	1	0
White female	Black female	0	0
Total		16	21
		(12 episodes)	(13 episodes)

Source: See appendix B.
1. One not guilty by reason of insanity.

pressed condition of most of the city's blacks created an active criminal or semicriminal class.[78] Five of those hanged for killing whites were convicted of robbery. More importantly, the figures in Table 17 reflect the fact that the illicit activities that figured prominently in black neighborhoods attracted a mixed clientele. Prostitution is always a dangerous trade, and it appears that some of the white female victims in the table were murdered by black pimps. By the evidence, troublesome customers were even more vulnerable, and nineteenth-century juries were not sympathetic, in retrospect, to victims who had been looking for action in strange neighborhoods.

The proportion of black women accused of homicide, within as well as across racial lines, was higher than that of white women. Some of those accused were prostitutes, but it is hard to tell how many, as others were brought to trial following incidents in which they were apparently protecting themselves from male harassment. Still other cases resulted from situations in which sex was irrelevant. Indeed that is one of the most important differences revealed by the series: the greater activity and wider range of roles played by black women as compared to white. The difference between white and black homicide rates among females was far greater than among males. While blacks cumulatively made up 4.3 percent of the city's population between 1839 and 1901, the 116 identifiable black males amounted to a little more than 10 percent of all males indicted, and the 33 black women accounted for nearly 26 percent of all women. Even more strikingly, black women were much more likely to play an aggressive role. While more than twice as many white women were victims (210) as accused killers (90), black women were more often killers than victims, although only by the insignificant margin of 33 to 29. The difference, moreover, would be accentuated if, as in the comparison between nineteenth- and twentieth-century women, the rather special crime of infanticide were omitted.

As indicated, some of the disparity between black and white women seems related to a difference in the nature of sex roles in the two communities. The materials from courts and newspapers suggest that black behavior patterns were much less segregated sexually than those of whites. White killings inside as well as outside the group often occurred during all-male brawls or as a result of encounters among small bands of roisterers on the move. Blacks were more restricted in their movements, because most of the city was white and dangerous at night. And the black population had its own divisions, such as the sometimes murderous enmity between uptown "Woodcocks" and downtown "Skinners."[79] More black killings occurred at home or near home; fewer were sparked at exclusively masculine gathering places, such as saloons. The sexes drank together, and most of the popular recreations that DuBois lists—from church suppers and excursions through balls and parties—virtually demanded the presence of both.[80] Women figured also in more serious, even deadly serious, activities, such as the territorial riot in which two women and just one man were indicted for beating a white stranger to death.[81]

Although much of the material from court, health, and coroner's records is evidence of the characteristically strong behavior of black women, some of it is evidence merely of desperation or of violence, especially of violence associated with family life or its absence. Since the history and structure of the black family has long been a matter of scholarly interest and more recently of public debate, the matter requires at least some mention here.

The older view, that plantation slavery allowed little room for the development of married life and kinship ties, has been discredited entirely. Eugene Genovese and Herbert Gutman, among others, have demonstrated the strength of nuclear two-parent families as well as wider supportive networks of relatives.[82] The evidence about free blacks, however, especially in northern cities after the Civil War, is relatively scant.[83] So is the relevant material in this study; the numbers are not large, and the angle of vision is obviously too grotesque to permit any generalizations about family life. But there are at least two sets of clues that may contribute to the continuing search for information in this area as well as to the more immediate purposes of this study. On the surface both sets tend to fit into the traditional picture of family weakness and instability drawn by scholars such as DuBois and E. Franklin Frazier. Neither, however, supports their analysis in full, and the second can be explained in a rather different way.

The first set of clues is provided by the figure for "unknown infants" found in the *Annual Register of Deaths*, as described above. The health office was not always careful about noting racial differences in these hopeless cases, which affected no one's heirs and no one's ancestors; color, and virtually all else, was legally as well as medically irrelevant. In some years no blacks at all were recorded; it is impossible to tell whether this means that none were found or simply that none were noted. But at times, especially in the years just after the Civil War, the totals include an inordinate number of black infants. In 1869, the highest year, 49 were reported, more than one-third of the 145 for the whole city and roughly ten times what proportionate numbers would suggest.

What these small bodies represent is no more clear for blacks than for others. Some slight evidence, most of it negative, suggests that blacks had less access to or were more wary of abortionists than whites, and thus may have brought more unwant-

ed pregnancies reluctantly to term. Certainly a greater proportion were domestic servants who stood to lose employment if
forced to raise a child. But in any case the figures, at least for
those years in which race was noted, do not indicate the existence of wide supportive family networks for these young
women, or indeed of that relative tolerance for illegitimacy
which was once counted as compensation for alleged weaknesses in family structure.

Comparatively few black women, just twelve of the thirty-
three indicted between 1839 and 1901, were brought to court for
infanticide. That is a considerably smaller proportion of all indictments than among white females. On the other hand, the
proportion of black women brought in for killing adults further
confirms their more active role. But this violence was itself part
of a larger pattern of black homicides, by both sexes, associated
with family or sexual problems. Collectively these killings constitute the second set of clues to consider. A somewhat larger
proportion of blacks (27 percent) than of whites (21 percent)
was indicted for killing relatives—uncles, parents, and inlaws,
as well as spouses and children—despite the fact that a smaller
proportion of the black population was married.[84] Impossible
to quantify but almost certainly sharper is the difference in the
white and black totals arising from sexual jealousy and tension.

It should be emphasized, however, that these figures do not
necessarily demonstrate anything about the nature of family
structure. Alternative explanations are suggested by the conditions described above, the often claustrophobic nature of black
living and recreational patterns, the fact that in the absence of
all-male drinking and socializing the sexes were more often together on potentially violent occasions. Most importantly,
whatever the relative incidence of domestic or related disputes,
black men and women were, for good reason, more likely than
whites to have weapons at hand.

Before the availability of revolvers, when firearms were both
clumsy and expensive, they were apparently even less common
among blacks than whites. The first black indictment for a
shooting death was not recorded until 1855, and there were
only two prior to 1870. But the black population was always

well armed. Even before 1867, the proportion of black killings with knives or other sharp instruments was greater than that of whites with guns and knives together. The habit of carrying pistols escalated toward century's end, and for the sixty-three years as a whole the combined total of homicides with weapons was 63 percent for blacks, 46 percent for whites.

The existence of a weapons culture clearly had an impact on many aspects of life within the black community. Its origins, and those of the habit of violence in general, go back before the beginning of this study; the black homicide rate was already considerably higher than the white in 1839-1845 and remained higher even in terms of killings without weapons. But it would seem that to explain this pattern in terms of family or indeed anything internal to the community is to reverse cause and effect. Forced out to the margins of the urban economy, living in or close to centers of criminal activity, subject to harassment outside of their own neighborhoods and sometimes to invasion, even armed mob invasion, inside of them, many blacks found eternal battle-readiness an essential survival mechanism.

What cheap handguns did to this cultural pattern was simply to intensify it, enabling an escalation in the rate of violence directed inside as well as outside of the group. And, what is critically important, there was nothing at work within the black community—unlike the white—to check the upward curve. While homicide rates in the city as a whole were dropping late in the century, the rate among the black community continued to rise, even though that community became larger, more nearly self-contained, and less threatened from without. The rate for 1839-1859, already high at 6.1 per 100,000, grew to 7.2 per 100,000 during 1860-1880, and to 9.3 during 1881-1901.

Most strikingly, this rise during the nineteenth century may be projected ahead into the late twentieth. As demographic change has made Philadelphia an increasingly black city, the black homicide rate in itself is enough to account for the differences between the overall official rates for 1839-1901, 1948-1952, and 1972-1974. Indeed the rising black homicide rate has obscured the contrary trend among whites, perhaps the most significant of all comparisons over time. Within the white population over the last two decades, escalating sales of handguns and the flight from the city of the richer, more educated, and less violent have combined to drive up the rates. But the long-term movement has been down. Chapter 4 records this phenomenon for the period 1839 to 1901; Table 18 demonstrates that even according to the "official" figures, with all of their inaccuracies, the white rate in this decade has only just crept back up to what it averaged throughout the nineteenth century.

Table 18. Black and white homicide rates per 100,000 population in 3 periods.

Color	1839-1901	1948-1952	1972-1974
Black	7.5	24.6	64.2
White	2.8	1.8	2.8

Source: See appendix B and notes 3 and 4 to chapter 5; also Wolfgang, *Homicide*, p. 66.

In sum, it is hard to compare the overall incidence of homicide across three or more generations, but after analysis of the figures it is possible to make at least some generalizations. The officially recorded rate of homicide in the modern city is much higher than that for nineteenth-century Philadelphia; moreover were it possible to discount the effects of improved medical technology, the contrast would be greater. On the other hand, if the object is to use killings as the most measurable index of violent behavior, then every other factor that bears on the number of homicides officially counted would, if adjusted for, increase the totals for the nineteenth century more than for the twentieth. Apart from the knotty and perhaps distinct problem of infanticide, these factors include the differing availability or use of firearms, the inherent gap between arrest and indictment as measures of homicide, and most important, given the ineffectuality of the nineteenth-century justice system at every level, the pressure to minimize the count at the first, or inquest, level.

Some of the characteristics of homicide in the previous century help to indicate why the rates were so consistently undercounted. But most significant are those factors that help to explain not only the deficiencies of the official rate but also the direction of the "real" one. Perhaps more than any other data, the differences among ethnic and racial groups, differences that imply much about such other matters as occupation and status, help to explain the connection among homicide, accident, and suicide, and to relate all three to the transformation of the city.

CHAPTER 6

CONCLUSION

The city of Philadelphia in the nineteenth century was part of a larger social and economic system that acted continuously to reshape the behavior of the urban population as a whole. The changing industrial city in fact "worked" in a variety of ways that the Chicago sociologists misinterpreted and that historians have not sufficiently appreciated. At the same time it failed to work in ways that have become increasingly apparent ever since.

These and other conclusions are supported by the mass of numbers used to represent the rates of violent death. In themselves, however, the eighteen tables so far presented, even with the four yet to come, can only demonstrate that change occurred, not how or why it happened. What is required is an explanation that links the several sets of materials presented and relates this result in turn to more fundamental processes affecting the lives of people in the city. The first step is to establish a connection among the indices of suicide, homicide, and accident, to make a single coherent pattern that makes sense both psychologically and statistically out of three separate ones. The next step is to relate this pattern to specific developments in Philadelphia and elsewhere in a way that interprets the connection between growth and violence more usefully than either of the traditional versions outlined in chapter 1. Beyond that the evidence from this study does not go. But it is possible, even ir-resistible, to speculate further, to suggest the ways in which the contemporary urban situation grew out of and differs from the experience of the past.

There are two ways in which the indices of vio-lent death can be linked. One is intrinsic, a relationship suggest-ed by the shape and nature of the statistical data themselves; the other is psychological, a theory that illumines and explains that relationship.

The most striking clue to the existence of a link among the separate trends in violent death is their timing, the fact that so far as can be determined, all of them appear to break, to change angle or direction, at roughly the same time. This is clearest in the case of suicide, which turns out rather surprisingly to be the index most easily measured over time. After a long period of stability, the suicide index (see Table 2) breaks upward in the middle, or fifth, of the nine seven-year periods, that is, some-time around 1870.

This break is not so apparent in the case of accident, but only because most accident rates are bound up with technological development in ways that are virtually impossible to disentan-gle before that same middle period. After that point, when the rate is disentangled, it moves steadily down. And in the one case—drowning—in which technology does not complicate the rates, the break is as clear as with suicide: after an equally long period of relative stability there is a sharp downturn, at almost the same angle at which suicide turns up (see Table 5).

The homicide index is the most complex—and least signifi-cant in terms of numbers—but although it is less pronounced, the break is there too. Before 1870 the homicide rates move down but only erratically (see Table 13). Afterward, from the early 1870s to the end of the century, the drop is steady and pronounced, especially when considered in light of the changing threshold of tolerance.

For at least a generation, since Andrew Henry and James Short published *Suicide and Homicide*, social scientists have intermittently investigated possible correlations between the rates of these two phenomena. One of them, social psychologist Martin Gold, has developed a simple theory that, with slight modification, fits and explains the differing patterns shown by the Philadelphia materials, including those for accident.

As several scholars have pointed out, a central problem with Durkheim's key concept of anomie, as originally formulated, was that it could as easily be used to predict homicidal as suicidal tendencies within a given group without specifying which to expect.[1] It is, however, easy to show that groups and societies with high rates of one often have low rates of the other. Henry and Short, using vital statistics from the United States, argued that the key to this difference was social status, and they proposed a simple dichotomy: suicide was behavior generally associated with persons of high status, homicide with persons of low status.[2] But while this theory explained some salient differences, such as those between whites and blacks, or rich and poor, it left others unaccounted for, such as those between the sexes. It was and is true that men, who have in our society generally higher status than women, do have higher rates of suicide, but they have higher rates of murder, also, and the difference between the sexes in this respect is even greater.

Gold's contribution is nearly as simple as Short's and Henry's but has the distinct advantage of encompassing not merely some but all of the variations among groups.[3] His starting point is not sociological but psychological, specifically the basic frustration-aggression hypothesis. Suicide and homicide are linked in that both are manifestations of aggression, in the first case directed inward, in the second, outward. Working out from psychology into sociology, he reasons that the "choice" between the two is conditioned by the individual's characteristic modes of expressing frustration or controlling aggression, which, in the aggregate, is the product of the social training of the group to which the individual belongs. Thus the socialization of aggression among class or ethnic subgroups differs in such a way as to incline them in different directions. The difference may indeed be expressed numerically, in terms of a "suicide-murder ratio," or SMR, obtained by dividing the suicide rate by the sum of both rates. Groups with low ratios, such as blacks, tend disproportionately to commit homicide, while those with high ratios, such as upper-status whites, tend to commit suicide. Moreover, to distinguish his theory further from that of Short and Henry, Gold points out that some groups simply exhibit higher levels of aggression than others, as males compared to females. In such cases, whatever the ratio expressed as a single number, the full formula, suicide rate ÷ (suicide rate + homicide rate), should show that both rates are higher in the more aggressive group.

In commonsense terms it is easy to fit accident into this simple model. The personal habits that may lead to manslaughter are essentially the same as those that lead to fatal accident: alcoholic recklessness, thoughtless reflex action, a challenge fiercely accepted on the riverbank or in the street. Gold finds that people inclined toward overt aggressiveness are "more spontaneous and expansive in their bodily expression of emotions"; modern research on accident victims finds them typically marked by "aggressive behavior, hyperactivity, and low tolerance to frustration."[4] The suicidally inclined personality in contrast is self-controlled and introspective, perhaps repressed, not so readily involved in accident unless on purpose. In a large population, then, rates of accident ought to vary positively with those for homicide and negatively with those for suicide, as they do in late nineteenth-century Philadelphia.

Gold's thesis is especially useful in analyzing the Philadelphia data because group differences in all of these respects were sharper then than they are today. Homicide, as now, was characteristically associated with the poor, the unskilled, the young, and those otherwise regarded as having low status in our society. Studies over the past generation have indicated that many of those who now commit suicide share similar characteristics.[5] But it is noteworthy that older surveys, of early or midtwentieth-century rates, indicate that the divergence was once more clearly marked, that suicide was generally found more often among people of high status.[6] Similarly, before long exposure to the dominant culture had blurred their original distinctiveness, there was a clear difference between the city's two major foreign ethnic groups, the Germans with a high suicide-murder ratio, the Irish with a low. The contrast between the races was sharper also; while homicide rates among blacks and whites have continued to diverge very strongly, the high white suicide rate in the previous century and the almost infinitesimal rate recorded for blacks in the same era would make the difference in their SMRs, if calculable, even more dramatic.[7] And finally, the differences for both rates between the sexes among whites was very marked in a period in which role, status, and distinctions of all kinds were more sharply defined than they are in the late twentieth century.

What Gold's thesis does for all of these findings is collectively to reinforce them. As with the three component indices of accident, so with the group differences and indeed the three major indices themselves: the whole is greater than the sum of the parts. Each important component drawn from the data is confirmed by its complement, as suggested by the theory; as suicide goes up, homicide and accident go down. And each important trend over time is magnified when considered not alone but as part of a changing suicide-murder ratio, in which differences are greater than in any one index considered by itself.

All of this serves to explain why the various indices may be expected to differ among groups, and, given movement over time, which ones should move closer together and which apart. However, it supplies no answers to the critical historical questions: why should there be movement at all, and what made it happen?

The central fallacy of the older sociological version of the link between growth and violence should be apparent from the data already established. The fears of many nineteenth-century observers and of later academics were not only groundless but wholly misleading, in that the city was by their own standards "working" better as its population grew. The apparent increase of problem behavior of all sorts, as measured by the statistics of courts, jails, and almshouses, was not "real" but "official," the product of stricter standards more strictly enforced. The nature of the operations of the criminal courts suggests that social control was more firmly established in the late-century metropolis than it had been in the smaller city before the Civil War. Of the forms of behavior described in this study, only the rise in suicide rates can possibly be interpreted as evidence that the growth of the city was accompanied by social disintegration. And even suicide, which was somewhat more clearly an upper-status phenomenon in the nineteenth century than it has been since, is better read as an ironic index of civilization, the inevitable accompaniment of falling rates of external aggression.

The data do not in the same way contradict the historians' version of Philadelphia's history, which stresses the reestablishment of political and social control over a population wracked by ethnic and economic rivalries between the 1830s and the late 1850s. But the data do underline the inadequacy or incompleteness of this explanation.

Mob activity did in fact pose a threat to political stability in midcentury Philadelphia and continued to, down to the last antiblack election riot in the spring of 1871. It is equally evident that political developments and institutions contributed to the decline in intergroup violence. Some of these developments were purposefully directed to that end, notably the consolidation of the city and the establishment of the police in 1854 and the erosion of the power of the fire companies, which culminated in the abolition of the volunteer system at the end of 1870. Other developments, if not so purposeful, were at least as effective—possibly the channeling of intergroup hostilities into electoral politics, as a result of stronger party organization, certainly the outcome of the Civil War.

But changes in most of the behavior studied here show how little the deeper rhythms of personal life were affected by those public events that have traditionally been the stuff of history. Most of the major indices of violent death were wholly unaffected by any combination of political developments. The turbulence of the 1840s, 1850s, and 1860s contrasts with the stability of the suicide rate; the municipal tranquility of the decades at century's end seems equally unrelated to the decline in drownings. Perhaps the professional police, and political realignment, in working to contain the worst effects of intergroup hostility, had some effect on the declining rate of homicide. But no such explanation can be stretched to cover the continuing divergence between the suicide-murder ratios of blacks and whites, the rising levels of black violence, which countered the opposite trend among the majority.

The Gold thesis does suggest that the process of socialization, and particularly the socialization of aggression, is the area in which to look for a more comprehensive explanation. But beyond that, it offers nothing more specifically useful. Gold believes that parental discipline in early childhood is the most important influence in inclining a person toward either the internal control or the direct expression of aggressive emotions.[8] The use of external punishment in particular, he argues, helps incline a child toward direct or overt expression and a group toward a low SMR, while indirect, nonphysical sanctions incline a child or group in the opposite direction. This proposition has been criticized, however, and in any case its usefulness for historians is restricted by problems of evidence.[9] The data about child-rearing in the previous century are limited. And nothing known about it suggests a change sudden, strong, and wide enough to account for a marked shift in the vital statistics of a richly heterogeneous population.

If, however, the search for changes in the socialization process is extended beyond the home and beyond the early childhood years, it is possible to find an explanation. In the nineteenth century Philadelphia's growth and that of America's urban population generally was largely the result of what is loosely called the industrial revolution. The changes associated with this process affected virtually every aspect of life in the city. Most directly they affected habits of work; much of the social history of the early industrial revolution (and indeed the process of development anywhere) can be written in terms of the transformation of a preindustrial into a modern work force.[10] What has not been understood for the United States is the way in which that transformation affected ordinary behavior of all kinds, including—perhaps especially—the behavior reflected in the indices of violence.

What is most demanded of a modernizing society is "predict-

ability in the behavior and relationships of individuals," or orderly cooperation at work.[11] The rhythms of the agricultural
year change continually, periods of intense activity alternating
with long slack seasons, and except at harvest there are few
chores that cannot be interrupted for an encounter, an adven-
ture, or simply a distraction. The same is true of the older traditional urban economy organized around independent crafts and
commerce. Few enterprises in early nineteenth-century Philadelphia employed more than a handful of workmen, each of
them relatively unspecialized, their pace and hours of employment regulated by the variable flow of specific orders. The work
force late in the century operated, in contrast, under a much
tighter set of constraints. Bell, clock, and foreman enforced a
degree of discipline that, if not harsher, was more nearly unre-
mitting than earlier. The need to coordinate specialized individual tasks with those of large numbers of fellows in factory or
office demanded synchronization and cooperation. The hours
and the nature of the job prohibited the easy workaday consumption of liquor and put a premium on the ability to endure
long stretches of frustration and boredom.[12]

The habits enforced at work were not confined to those people who were directly exposed to industrial or bureaucratic discipline. The process of socialization should be regarded as
broad and continuous, affecting behavior that is not inculcated
specifically and going on throughout the span of life. Living in
the city is itself an education. Erving Goffman has shown repeatedly that a dense or urban population acquires a great variety of behavioral norms learned by some process of example or
contagion that operates well below the level of rational consciousness.[13] Adults exposed to the same environment over time
act in broadly similar fashion, no matter what their individual
early or childhood experiences.

For children in late nineteenth-century America, the requisite
learning process often began in the growing system of public
schools. It is not simply that the public schools operated as gen-
eralized agents of social control: quite specifically, the kinds of
behavior they inculcated were those demanded by the changing
economy. Samuel Bowles and Herbert Gintis have found that
the drive for public schooling was strongest in communities in

which there was a heavy demand for semiskilled manufacturing employment.[14] Even apart from literacy, which had earlier been learned in a variety of less structured ways, the consciousness of bell, clock, and deadline, the self-discipline required to sit still, take turns, and mind the teacher, were well designed to prepare students for life in office or factory. Public education was in that sense fully relevant; the lessons of school and workplace naturally reinforced each other.

As agencies of socialization, in Gold's terms, both school and workplace were teaching behavior that would affect the suicide-murder ratio and the accident rate in just the manner indicated by the Philadelphia statistics of violent death.[15] Although the specific mechanisms cited by Gold may be inapplicable to this study, there is no reason to doubt his analysis of the opposing patterns of expression that distinguish the homicidally from the suicidally inclined. The former are those whose training "does not build in controls over direct expression," and the words used to describe them, such as "impulsive" and "spontaneous," indicate precisely the qualities repressed or redirected in school or factory.[16] Research among modern children, too, has found that rates of accident are quite directly related to the degree of resistance to the classroom, with a list of ten characteristics including "fights with peers," "discipline problems," "impulsiveness," and "careless, unreliable" as the most related, and "good school achievement" as the least.[17] Gold describes those who have a statistically greater tendency toward suicide in exactly opposite terms, as model students, "children of the bureaucratic middle class," preparing for a life in which "economic success rests heavily on the development of harmonious social relations," and in which overt aggressiveness is deplored.[18]

In theory, then, the effects of the industrial revolution might account in a crudely behavioral way for the changing habits measured in the indices of violent death. It remains to show how well such a theory fits the information available.

Even if the mechanisms of "socialization" were better understood, and the term itself more precise, the kaleidoscopic nature of the varied and always shifting population of nineteenth-century Philadelphia would make generalization difficult. Only a minority of adult residents, at any given time, had been born in the city. The others were raised in a range of environments—New England farms, Rhineland villages, cottages in the West of Ireland—which had little in common except for the fact that they did little directly to prepare their residents for life in a great industrializing metropolis. It cannot be argued that the impact of parallel experiences in school or at work was as important in shaping behavior patterns as differences in cultural background or sex. Different people and groups were unevenly exposed to these experiences and reacted differently to them. Moreover, the evidence for the impact of industrial discipline is blunted not only by the variety of people's backgrounds but by specific deficiencies in the available data. But cumulatively the data do strongly support the thesis that the decline in violently reckless behavior was a product of the discipline demanded by the industrial revolution and taught in the classrooms, on the railroads, and in the factories and offices of nineteenth-century America.

The evidence is of three kinds: the timing of mass exposure to new influences in school and at work, the differing occupational and work habits of those who committed suicide and those who committed homicide, and the continuing divergence between the suicide-homicide ratios of blacks and whites.

Since the great majority of adult Philadelphians were educated elsewhere if at all, it would be emphasis misplaced to recount the history of the city's public school system or even that of the Commonwealth of Pennsylvania as a whole. Given the extraordinary geographical mobility of nineteenth-century Americans, the scope of inquiry must be as wide as possible, and all that can be said is that the information available does suggest that the period around 1870 should mark a turning point.

It was in 1870 precisely that the United States Commissioner of Education began to issue national statistics, a series that indicates the same steadiness of direction as those for violent death. The percent of eligible children in school and average number of days attended show virtually uninterrupted progress, with the former figure moving from 57 percent in 1870 to a little over 72 percent by 1901, and the latter moving from seventy-eight to ninety-nine days.[19] There is no nationwide information for any period before that date, but in general terms the history of the public school movement is well known. The key battles were fought during the 1840s; most of the northern and western states adopted systems of free, compulsory, tax-supported schools during the 1850s. By 1860 in these areas, more than half of the eligible population was being exposed to formal educational discipline.[20] Children in the nineteenth century did not, however, figure importantly in the statistics that make up the suicide-murder ratio. It was in the late 1860s and early 1870s that this crucial first generation of the publicly educated entered young adulthood, to be followed in unbroken succession, and increasing proportion, by those after.

Equivalent figures do not exist for the impact of socialization on the job. While it may be assumed that public-school children were exposed to broadly similar systems of educational discipline, there was far more variety in the workplace. As in education, where the issue is not the production of literates but the means of their production, so at work the issue is not what goods or services were produced but under what conditions. White-collar workers were by definition people who had learned enough control to receive an education and to behave predictably, but relative status below the traditional "collar line" is no sure evidence of a disciplined socialization. A man skilled in a traditional craft was rated more highly than a semiskilled factory operative in the same industry but was subject to less external restraint if working alone or in a small group. It was after all men from the traditional handicraft sectors of Philadelphia's economy who joined the battling gangs and fire companies that enlivened the streets during the 1840s and 1850s and continue to enliven the histories of that violent era.[21]

It is not easy to determine which specific jobs were most successful in conditioning or regimenting those who managed to hold them, but two statements can be made with confidence. One is that the habits of order and regularity were most likely to be inculcated in people working in bureaucracies or in estab-

lishments that employed a significant number of people working together under close supervision. The other is that national
statistics show that the largest proportional gains in these kinds
of employment, trade, service, and manufacture were made in
the decade just before 1870.[22]

Unfortunately the statistics for accidental death cannot be
used to support this thesis for three reasons. One is that as explained in chapter 2 on suicide, the registration of occupations
in the *Annual Register of Deaths* is not fully trustworthy. Moreover, death from accident is more complicated than suicide or
homicide in that it is often not the responsible agent but the un-
witting victim of some careless mishap whose name is entered
in the book. Finally, job-related changes in personal behavior
were matched or overmatched by the increasing dangers posed
by the impersonal behavior of the machines that defined the age
of industry. The most demanding and disciplined occupations
were often the most deadly. The toll exacted by the Pennsylvania Railroad or among the employees at Cramp's Shipyard cannot all be laid to the recklessness of individual victims, men
who might have lived longer in the more leisurely environment
of traditional work.

The available figures for suicide and homicide, however,
while complicated, and not well fitted to answer the relevant
questions with precision, do provide strong evidence about the
relationship between occupation and behavior. Much basic information about the status and occupations of nineteenth-
century suicides has been given in chapter 2. Overwhelmingly
white males, generally of higher than average status if immigration is discounted, they typically were or had been deeply involved in the social economy of the city. But the figures compiled by Dr. Billings for the census of 1890 reveal much more
than this.[23] High income or status correlates only very roughly
with suicide; neither is a truly useful predictor of the age-standardized rates shown in Table 19.

None of the usual indices of class or prestige can be used to
explain the findings in this table. The line between men with
high and low rates does not cleanly divide rich from poor, white
collar from blue, or the self-employed from the wage-earning.

Table 19. Age-standardized suicide rates for all occupied males over
15 in registration states of 1890 census.

Occupation	Number (in 1,000s)	Suicide rate
Above average rate		
Personal service, police and military	78	28.6
Professional	117	23.7
Clerical and official	324	21.2
Laboring and servant	469	17.6
Manufacturing and mechanical	1,168	17.0
Average rate for all occupied	3,491	15.6
Below average rate		
Entertainment	55	12.9
Mercantile and trading	291	12.7
Agriculture, transport, other outdoor	990	10.4

Source: U.S. Census of 1890; see chapter 2.

The lack of information about a number of variables—perhaps
most important, the ethnic or cultural background of those employed—prevents any absolute generalizations. But given the
available information, the best divider is none of the lines above
but rather one that cuts across all of them. It separates those
men, low in suicide, whose work was largely self-directed, unevenly paced, and performed alone or in small groups, from
those, high in suicide, whose work demanded formal education,
or close supervision, or both. More briefly, the division is between the old and the new styles of work.

This conclusion becomes clearer when the broad categories in
the table are analyzed further. At the bottom end of the suicide
scale, among the subgroups in the most traditional category,
"agriculture, transportation, and other outdoor occupations,"
there was relatively little variation.[24] Among substantial subgroups at the top, the list was led, as all social observers might
predict, by "bankers, brokers, and officials of companies," with
age-adjusted rates of 27.1 per 100,000. In second place, how-

ever, were the classically repressed bureaucrats par excellence, the lowly "accountants, bookkeepers, clerks, and copyists," at 23.8; lawyers stood third at 22.6. In the "laboring and servant" class, the laborers pulled up the group—servants were quite low—perhaps because so many were recent immigrants as well as men who tended increasingly to work in large supervised groups.[25] The "entertainment" category, with its low rates, consisted entirely of small owners or operators, "keepers of hotels and boarding houses," "saloon keepers, restaurant keepers, bartenders, etc." These men practiced their ancient trade at the same irregular pace as their convivial customers, the "commercial travellers and salesmen," "hucksters and peddlers," who made up much of the "mercantile and trading" class. Cabinetmakers, traditional aristocrats of the "manufacturing and mechanical" category, stood very close to its low end, at 9.4, just above the biggest subcategory, the skilled and relatively well-paid "carpenters and joiners," at 8.8. Machinists, however, stood at 19.1, and no group of comparable size rivaled the rate of those engaged in the newest and most supervised of manual occupations, the "mill and factory operatives," at 21.0.

The situation of those men accused of homicide was very different. If suicides tended to belong to the most modern sectors of the economy, the situation of murderers was much more precarious. And while some of the relevant information is incomplete, the fact of incompleteness is itself a form of evidence.

The job listings for adult males indicted for first-degree murder, as available, indicate that these men were typically of lower status than either suicides or the general population. The group considered here, which excludes all who were apparently under fifteen years old, inmates of prisons and asylums, and those whose cases failed to reach the courtroom, consists of 881 of the males indicted between 1839 and 1901.[26] The occupations of those whose names, jobs, and addresses were listed in the series of annually published city directories may be compared with the jobs held by male Philadelphians generally in 1880, as estimated from the federal census.[27] This procedure indicates, not surprisingly, that accused murderers were less likely than the control group to be white collar or skilled and more likely to be semiskilled, service, or unskilled workers.[28] But it would be misleading to describe the nature of their work in more detail; what was found about jobs is less important than what was not found, for fewer than one-third, just 264 of the 881 men, can be located in the directories at all.

It is not known with certainty why some men were listed in this series and others not, but Stephan Thernstrom has suggested the apparent criterion for the very similar Boston directories.[29] The principle of inclusion, he finds, was not class or status, although the effect was that a higher proportion of high- than of low-status persons were listed, but rather apparent permanence of residence, an individual's evident intention to stay in the city for a time and thus in effect to advertise his presence and occupation. The directories of both cities included a large number of poor men, common laborers; what they omitted were transients, bachelor occupants of hotels and boarding-houses, men who seemed unlikely to settle in. The total number of adult males counted in late-century Boston was about 75 percent of all who were located in the city at a given time.[30] This figure is cumulatively about right for Philadelphia, although it varied, and increased, over time. Allowing something more than 10 percent for the proportion of men between fifteen and twenty years old, this means that some 65 percent of all who were fifteen and over should be listed. Before the consolidation of 1854, the percentage was markedly lower than it was later, in part because the listings included residents of the city only, and not those of the county as a whole. In any case the number of names included, as a percentage of males fifteen and over in Philadelphia County, may be estimated at 51 percent for the directory of 1840; 38 percent for 1850; 64 percent for 1860; 79 percent for 1870; 68 percent for 1880; 66 percent for 1890; and 70 percent for 1900.[31]

These figures for the general male population contrast strongly with those for the men tried for murder. Among this group the percentage found in the directories, during the year of or year prior to their indictments, is shown in Table 20. These figures do not reveal anything directly about employment, but they suggest much, quite directly, about lifestyle and behavior.

Table 20.   Percentages of adult males tried for murder and found in
Philadelphia city directories for 3 periods.

Years	Not listed	Unclear	Total found
1839-1859	53	13	34
1860-1880	49	19	33
1881-1901	41	30	29

Source: See appendix B.

Although, strictly speaking, nothing can be said about those not listed, it is apparent that they were mostly men of few or no skills, some of them involved in illicit enterprises, living in places easily overlooked or perhaps hidden. The "unclear" group seems to have shared these characteristics to an even greater degree. These were men with common names, so that more than one appears in the directory, or whose names were somewhat garbled, for whom the *Ledger* listed no occupation or specific address at all. (A few, for example, were "said to live in a place called 'twelve-foot alley.' ") These omissions would be unlikely except for men who had undistinguished jobs or none, and who lacked families, customers, or neighbors to supply or to be concerned about such specific information.

American cities have always contained large numbers of mobile people; the "persistence rate," or percentage of male adults who typically stayed in a single place for a full decade, seems over the past century and a half to have remained quite constant at somewhere between 40 percent and 60 percent of the population.[32] There is no reason to suppose that the figure should change if the "male adult" category is, as here, extended to include those fifteen and older. In any case, if these people, the relatively permanent residents, are envisioned as islands anchored in a stream of migrants, then Philadelphia's murderers overwhelmingly were men whose real home was in the stream. Even among the minority who can be found in the directories, only a little over a quarter were listed for as long as four years, roughly half as many as those who, in the general population, persisted for ten. Homicide was then largely associated with the class of transients, drifters, and newcomers to the city.[33]

One more table confirms the suggestion that Philadelphia's nineteenth-century murderers were typically marginal men, those left behind by or new to the demands for order and discipline. One of the rhythms of the new economic order, felt more keenly than in the old, was the pattern imposed by the work week. Regular, continuous, supervised work, ten or twelve hours a day, six days out of seven, left little time free for trouble. It also heightened the contrast between Saturday night, the following Sunday, and the rest of the week. Earlier work patterns, with less insistence on set times and more breaks during the day, left more time to drink, socialize, and quarrel all the week through. In a world thoroughly "broken" to industrial rhythms there is for workingmen a relatively quiet period from Monday through payday, which was Saturday in the nineteenth century, Friday by the midtwentieth, followed by intensive and potentially explosive activity until the round begins again. This situation is reflected in the homicide statistics for Philadelphia in 1948-1952, a time of full employment, when after a century of experience with industrialism and bureaucracy, even those groups not directly affected were conditioned by their schedules. For the previous century, however, even though the weekend was not two days but only one, the Saturday peak was far less sharp, and murder was spread more evenly through the week, as shown in Table 21. The hard beat of the new work rhythms was still heard only faintly by those who accounted for most of the city's violence.

The most violent group of all, finally, was the one least touched directly by the industrial revolution, the one left farthest behind.

Even more than bureaucracy, more than schooling, industrial employment in the nineteenth century was reserved for white men. In Philadelphia as nationally, black men in the second half of the century were not only confined to the most casual and irregular work but were losing what foothold they had earlier secured in better-paying jobs. By the late 1890s DuBois found that three-quarters of all employed blacks in the seventh ward were

Table 21.   Percentages of murders committed by day of the week, 1839-
1901 and 1948-1952.

Years	Mon.	Tues.	Wed.	Thurs.	Fri.	Sat.	Sun.
1839-1901[1]	14	14	12	9	12	21	17
1948-1952	10	7	9	8	17	32	17

Source: See appendix B, and Wolfgang, *Homicide,* p. 107.
1. Percentages for cases coming to trial only.

either servants or laborers, and that while "for years the Negro
filled satisfactorily the trades of the city," as time passed "in
Philadelphia a determined prejudice, aided by public opinion,
has succeeded nearly in driving them from the field."[34] Only a
little over 8 percent of blacks, as compared to nearly 47 percent
of the city's working population as a whole, were "engaged in
manufacturing and mechanical industries"; virtually none of
these worked in factories but rather plied traditional trades,
many threatened with obsolescence.[35] "White workingmen,"
DuBois concluded, "have . . . monopolized the new industrial
opportunities of an age which has transformed Philadelphia
from a colonial town to a world city."[36]

It cannot be argued that the level of violence in the black
community was wholly the result of patterns of employment or
schooling. In every group a range of cultural patterns asserted
themselves in many ways. With respect specifically to the suicide-murder ratio, it is obvious that the immigrant Irish, Germans, Italians, Poles, and Jews all reacted differently to conditions in the same city. Analysis of the cultural elements that did
or did not incline members of each group toward the external
expression of aggression lies beyond the scope of this study.
Among blacks, however, John Dollard and more recently
Charles Silberman have found a great range of elements tending
toward violence, some of them the result of special insecurities
and frustrations, others integral to a subculture that, especially
for young males, has placed a special value on verbal and physical aggression.[37] It appears, however, that this "subculture of
violence" is almost wholly the product of American conditions

and, both before and after the Civil War, of conditions experienced outside of slavery.[38] Although the particular manifestations of the subculture, from the apotheosis of the mythical Stagolee to the practice of "playing the dozens" on street corners, have been developed and transmitted inside the group, much of the explanation for its origins, and especially its continuance, must be sought outside, in the conditions of and opportunities for work.

The high rate of homicide among blacks may be explained up to a point in purely instrumental terms, as was done at the end of chapter 5. There was a clear need, very early, for members of Philadelphia's black community to carry weapons and be ready to use them. It is equally clear that this need was in turn related directly and indirectly to problems of employment. Commercial vice and crime, occupations found for want of better ones, not only created a routinely dangerous habitat for those surrounded by them but also reinforced the prejudices and hostilities of the dominant whites who repeatedly invaded black neighborhoods in gangs. If the black murder rate in the 1840s and 1850s was high, it was not dramatically higher than that among the Irish at the same time or the Italians two generations later. If the high rate was both produced by and contributed to a subculture that encouraged the violent expression of aggression, that too might be said of the Irish or Italians. What must be explained is not the initial level but the fact that this level continued to rise among blacks while it fell among white immigrants.

The rising rate of black violence may perhaps be explained partly by rising frustration, as the promise of freedom was never realized, as escape from bondage and tenantry in the South led only to discrimination and poverty in the North. It may also be explained, in part, as in chapter 5, by the increasing availability of firearms. But the guns were equally available to all groups. And the point about anger or frustration, in terms of the suicide-murder ratio, is not just how intensely it was felt but rather how it was expressed.

Among other groups, over time, fewer individuals were inclined to the kind of reckless aggression of which homicide is the extreme expression. Only those newly arrived, perhaps, or the congenitally restless or resistant typically failed to meet the demands of the industrial age. The blacks, uniquely, were left behind as a group. They continued, uniquely, to express themselves in the old way in a new world. And without external checks to redirect it, the habit of violence continued to escalate as time moved them farther toward the margins of the industrial economy.

The experience of nineteenth-century Philadelphia is no sure guide to more recent developments. But while it is impossible to project that experience with any certainty across three crowded generations, an attempt to apply the analysis above may help to illumine the nature and causes of modern urban violence in America.

No published study has analyzed homicide or suicide rates as thoroughly as this one for any considerable period of the twentieth century. The existing official figures from several sources tend to show an increase in homicide, nationally, during the first two or three decades.[39] But it is not clear how much of this rise is "real" rather than merely official, the product of influences similar to those examined in chapters 4 and 5. These influences include, in addition to simple improvements in reportage: a continuance of high late-century standards of prosecution and low tolerance for violence; automobile accidents cited as manslaughter or even murder; more firearms; the continued influx of foreign and domestic black immigrants with high rates; changing patterns in homicide, making it easier to "solve" cases; police forces equipped with telephones, automobiles, and new priorities with respect to the detection of murder. It is in any case significant that from 1933, when the Federal Bureau of Investigation began collecting its Uniform Crime Reports, to about 1960, the national trend was reportedly down.[40] Certainly after discounting the other factors affecting the reported homicide rates, the evidence agrees with the Philadelphia figures at the end of chapter 5: the homicide rate among urban white Americans fell, perhaps almost steadily, from the late nineteenth century until very recently, when shifting class and demographic patterns altered the composition of the urban white group. The same scattered evidence, to the extent that it deals with racial differences, suggests that nationally, as in Philadelphia, the black homicide rate has continued sharply to rise.

For much of this period of seventy-odd years the explanation offered in terms of nineteenth-century Philadelphia may be projected, without amendment, to account for the continuing divergence between the white and black rates. Very simply, while the effect of urban-industrial discipline was increasingly felt among whites, the absence of the same discipline was increasingly evident among blacks. Not until World War II ended the Great Depression were factory jobs, notably, opened generally to black workers.[41]

A somewhat more complex explanation, however, is required to account for changes in the index for suicide, as well as for ways in which developments of the past twenty years have affected the rates for homicide.

Current rates for suicide in Philadelphia by sex, age, and race, cannot, quite, be obtained simply by projecting the trends already evident in the nineteenth-century figures, but only a single adjustment is needed. What has happened, broadly, is that suicide has been in some sense "democratized," with rates for women, children, and blacks all continuing to rise between 1900 and 1970, just as they had been rising from about 1870 to 1900.[42] The only drop has occurred among adult white males. This may be attributed to the ending of immigration, which as shown in chapter 2, was heavily associated with suicidal behavior. Another factor may be the changing class composition of the white population, the result of the flight to the suburbs, which has also raised the rate for homicide among those whites remaining.

Rising suicides among minors, numerically the least dramatic among the three groups moving upward, is not explicable in terms of the relatively simple behaviorism used throughout this study and calls for more sophisticated social and psychological analysis.[43] The increase for women is doubtless related to the same social changes that have led to higher female homicide rates; the gap between men and women is closing in this respect among many. But the great rise in the black suicide rate, from a base which in nineteenth-century Philadelphia was too low to calculate, up to a level which now threatens to exceed the white rate, is a phenomenon that commands attention.

The economic and social experience of urban blacks since World War II has been much more complicated than it was earlier. Even apart from the spectacular mobility enjoyed by exceptional and well-publicized individuals, substantial gains have been made by a growing middle and upper middle class. At the same time a large and increasingly immobile lower class has remained, victims of a cruel irony of history. During the 1940s blacks were, in effect, piped aboard a sinking ship, winning access to industrial employment just before the heralded "postindustrial" era of the 1950s and after. The fortunate and better-educated were able to win jobs in the new economy; many were not. Although a weakened discrimination remains, the essential problem for blacks in the modern city has been rather the lack of the kind of employment that not only sustained but socialized the white immigrant groups of the nineteenth and early twentieth centuries.

The actual trends in homicide and suicide, in the aggregate, have been just what the theory outlined in the preceding sections would predict as a result of this diverging experience. The growing black middle class has been subject to influences, expectations, and pressures parallel to those on their white peers and complicated by others peculiar to their own unique situation. Traditional or subcultural behavior patterns may contribute to high levels of homicide, relative to those for whites; all else, including uniquely high levels of anxiety, would incline members of the middle class to rates of suicide higher than that for other blacks or generally for whites. Among the lower class, meanwhile, the continued and even growing level of underemployment or unemployment among young males has created an intolerable level of frustration, which is now often expressed internally as well as externally.

The soaring rise in black homicide has been documented often; in Philadelphia, as shown in Table 18, the black arrest rate for murder and manslaughter is more than twenty times that for whites. The phenomenon of black suicide is less well known. By 1949-1951 it had climbed to 5.4 per 100,000, on an age-adjusted basis, compared to 9.0 for whites. In 1969-1971 it had reached 10.4, as compared to 12.7. By the latter period, in fact, the black male rate had passed the rate for white males, 16.7 to 16.2.[44] But in a significant way the suicide phenomenon within each group continues to diverge. As Herbert Hendin noted a decade ago, the tendency to self-destruction among whites increases roughly with age, but black males are most suicidal in their twenties or even late teens.[45] This is precisely the most homicidally inclined age group as well, which starkly reveals the common denominator—the raging frustration—that underlines both kinds of behavior. Outward aggression, it must be remembered, is still by far the more common form of expression for these youths, and rising murder rates have kept the suicide-murder ratio much lower than among whites. But it appears that young black men suffer from the worst of both worlds and that their marginal position in the urban economy clearly contributes to an appalling death rate at their own hands as well as those of their fellows and peers.

In retrospect it appears that the 1948-1952 period covered by Marvin Wolfgang's study represents a kind of high point in the success of the urban-industrial revolution that began in the previous century. After the Second World War, before and during the Korean, in a period of prosperity and full employment, the urban-industrial economy was "working" better than ever before. The white population had long grown accustomed to its demands, and the black had real hopes of being included in its benefits.

Since then, however, the patterns of homicide in the post-industrial city of the 1960s and 1970s have reverted in many respects to those of the preindustrial city of the 1840s and 1850s. The presence of young men with much free time and little supervision, in an economic environment that has nothing productive for them to do, accounts for many similarities between the two periods. When either is compared with the years around 1950, it appears that there are more killings in the streets, more brawls and gang murders, a more marked disparity between male and female rates of homicide, more interracial homicides, more freedom from the constraints of the work week, less violence concentrated on Saturday nights.[46] The last phenomenon can be demonstrated most graphically when the figures for 1972-1974 are added to those just given for the two earlier periods, as shown in Table 22. Despite the framework provided by the weekday-weekend distinction in the wider society and the regular weekly arrival of checks in the inner city, one day looks much like another to those not working steadily.

Meanwhile both schools and police seem to have lost the respect and confidence of the population as a result of their apparent inability to deal with the situation. Both public schooling and professional policing were developed originally in the 1840s, just at the start of the urban-industrial age and served during a long painful period to help accustom the population to the demands of that age. Neither institution in its present form is in the same sense relevant in the postindustrial era. The virtues of orderly or middle-class behavior are not self-evident to young people exposed to modern excitements and expectations. In the absence of employment that demands these virtues, the attempt to impose them is inevitably resented as irrelevant, even tyrannical, and thus doomed to failure.

Much of the argument above must remain speculation until further research is done. This study is limited not only in time and place but in conception, involving only a few of the many elements that shape behavior. But despite this caveat, the experience of nineteenth-century Philadelphia does support a few firm generalizations about urban growth and violence.

That experience indicates first that if growth is defined simply in terms of population, there is no necessary connection between the two. The statistical indices of suicide, accident, and homicide, when carefully examined, prove to be useful tools of social analysis. Especially when linked together, as suggested by Gold's suicide-murder ratio, they may indicate much about the

Table 22.   Percentages of murders committed by day of the week, for
3 periods.

Years	Mon.-Thurs.	Fri.	Sat.	Sun.	Total weekend
1839-1901[1]	49	12	21	17	50
1948-1952	34	17	32	17	66
1972-1974	49	16	20	14	50

Source: Table 21, and Hartleroad study described in chapter 5, note 3.
1. Percentages for cases coming to trial only.

socialization of a whole population or any of a number of identifiable subgroups. But among the several influences that seem
to shape that ratio or to change the direction of its component
parts, neither the size of the city nor its rate of increase seems
especially important. While the curve of population was always
and sharply up, there was a long period of relative stasis in the
measurable indices of violent death; during the last thirty years
of the century, when the indices changed most dramatically, the
rate of population increase was slower than during the first thirty, when they did not.

Nothing in the entire sixty-three years of historical experience
was as important in shaping the characteristic suicide-murder
ratio of each subgroup as the initial "given" that defines it—sex,
class, nativity, or race. But changes in both suicide and homicide rates and in the allied indices for accident were all related to
one complex event, the growth of the industrial revolution,
whose progress directly or indirectly affected everyone in the
city.

The primary effect was simply to raise the aggregate SMR
and lower the propensity for accident among the whole population. The need for sober predictability was met, on the whole;
most residents of Philadelphia, whatever their origins, learned
in school, at work, or by example somehow to curb their aggressiveness or to redirect it inward. In its own terms, then, the
industrial city was working, becoming more orderly over time
as its work force became more efficient.

Articulate contemporaries did not always understand either

what was going on or why. Certainly the sociologists of the Chicago School did not; changes in behavior were obscured by changing standards of behavior as the threshold of tolerance of violence was lowered, and there were always problems to occupy the courts, fill the newspapers, and inflate the official statistics. It was true that the process of industrialization exacted a price, but that price was only partially perceived at the time.[47]

Some of the price was painful and obvious. Quite apart from the values placed on such words as "order" and "regimentation," "spontaneity" and "recklessness," the actual incidence of violent death over the entire period was not declining but growing. While Philadelphians were less inclined to behave in ways that courted accident, changes in domestic, industrial, and transport technology combined to increase the actual casualty rate between 1840 and 1900. And if, unnoticed, proportionately fewer people committed homicides, far more, and from a wider spectrum of the whole population, were impelled to commit suicide.

It was always apparent that change was a selective process, that the industrial revolution involved most but not all of the work force, and that those left behind were more and more out of step. Contemporaries worried much about the social problems posed by immigrants and transients, despite the economic function their mobility may have served. They were less sensitive to the unique situation of urban blacks, who were left out not by bad luck or choice but through deliberate discrimination. Increasingly frustrated and violent behavior in the black population could be overlooked so long as the system worked as a whole and so long as the blacks remained a relatively small minority in the city.

The nineteenth-century city, then, was only partially successful in imposing its demands upon the population that came to live in it. Now that the industrial city is dead or dying in this country, its successes are still overlooked, but the heritage of its failures remains and is in fact growing. Although cities need not be violent, they may be, perhaps especially in a time when the institutions of another era are no longer adequate or relevant to this one. The crowds are still with us, and the noise and dirt and smoke, which have always repelled observers. But while the age of industry is behind us as an economic system, we have yet to discover a functional substitute for it as a social system, something capable, ideally in a more humane and inclusive way, of providing order and opportunity for people who live in cities.

APPENDIX A

HISTORICAL SOURCES

The *Public Ledger*

Virtually all of the descriptive accounts of violent death in this book have been drawn from a single newspaper, the Philadelphia *Public Ledger*. Every issue of the *Ledger* for the years 1839, 1840, 1841, 1870, and 1900 was read systematically for material bearing on homicide, suicide, and accident. Other years were sampled, and certain singular events were checked specifically by date. Indeed, the availability of newspaper information helped to dictate the earlier boundary of the study. While 1901 simply marks the turn of the century, the decision to go no further back than 1839 was determined in part by the fact that local news in the *Ledger* was often inadequate before that year, when the format was revised.

While the statistics used in text and tables are presented simply so as to be accessible to all readers, the problems involved in gathering them were fairly complicated, and it is essential to render an accounting of my methods.

All figures and certainly vital statistics from another century should be approached with skepticism. It is simply not responsible to use them in argument without a short Discourse on Method, describing not only the precautions observed, pitfalls avoided, and residual doubts discounted, but the basic process of compilation itself. The precautions are described in the text when appropriate. Most of the information has been compiled from just two sources: Philadelphia's health office and the reports of the county coroners. The two are further linked in that in cases of violence the figures tabulated by the former were generally processed first by the latter. Both sources require some explanation, as do those for population figures and the measures taken to adjust or standardize them.

The Health Department

The board of health for the "City and Liberties" of Philadelphia, a jurisdiction that from the beginning was coterminous with the county, was established in 1806 principally to maintain a lazaretto, as well as to assure that disease was not imported from abroad and to maintain standards of cleanliness generally.[1] An act of 1818 expanded the duties of the board to include, among other tasks, the registration of all deaths, or more precisely all burials, in the county. Before disposing of a body, the sexton or undertaker was required to have a certificate signed by a physician, the coroner, or a member of the immediate family who had been in attendance at the last.[2] These death certificates, which were supposed to indicate name, age, and cause of death, were sent to the principal health officer, who edited and published them in the newspaper once a week. The major purpose of this was apparently to notify doctors of what diseases were going around; during the cholera epidemic of 1849, publication of the full death list was suspended while the officer concentrated on daily bulletins on the topic of immediate concern.

From a historian's point of view there are several flaws in the system as it operated in that period. The only means of obtaining death totals is to add up the weekly figures as published in the *Public Ledger.* The totals themselves are clearly too low; by 1860 there were 145 burying grounds in Philadelphia, and the keepers of some of the smaller ones, especially, were not always zealous in forwarding their paperwork.[3] Only after the slight tabular improvement offered in 1849 was it possible to distinguish between the number of adults and of minors buried weekly for each of the two or three dozen causes listed. No further refinements, such as distinction by sex, were published; the number of "people of color" and of almshouse patients were given, together with age ranges, but these were gross totals only. A total of seventeen weeks are missing from the list in the twenty-one years and six months between 1839 and the commencement of a new system in 1860. In 1853 and 1858 there are gaps of several weeks, during the transition from one health officer to another. For the text and tables, the figures for the equivalent weeks in the preceding year have been substituted for those missing.

This relatively primitive system was greatly improved beginning in 1860 when Philadelphia adopted the registration system that had been pioneered in London in 1837 and was subsequently adopted throughout the Western world.[4] Under the new law all death certificates had to be signed by a licensed physician, the coroner or a deputy, or the health officer himself; family signatories were no longer acceptable. Gathered weekly from the undertakers, as before, the new certificates provided more information than the old, including address, occupation (sometimes), place of birth, and marital status. Each death was individually registered in books open to the public, along with birth and marriage records kept by the health office, which was considerably expanded for the purpose. This manuscript register, alphabetized and later indexed, is cited in the text as *Annual Register of Deaths.* The totals were further subject to the nineteenth century's fascination with statistics; at the end of each year all deaths were sorted into a variety of tables that analyzed the data in dozens of ways and compared them with listings from dozens of places. These results were published in two series, as individual books and as part of the *Annual Addresses of the Mayors of the City;* both of these sources, although they sometimes differ slightly from each other, are cited in the text as *Annual Health Report,* with date.

Within a few years of its adoption it could be fairly said that the system was working well. In the period after reorganization, the board of health continually hounded the keepers of burial grounds and sometimes doctors to make sure that the counts were accurate, and the causes of death were given according to a standard classification scheme, "without the affectation of high-sounding words."[5] While the totals for violent death, processed through the coroner's office as before, did not seem affected by these improvements. the total number of all reported burials went up by about 10 percent, the board noted, as soon as the new system went into effect. The aggregate figures, which were more accurate than those for birth or marriage, by the late 1860s probably came close to measuring the real incidence of death in the city. Specific names and dates, moreover, if not always the other information, were accurately recorded in the *Annual Register of Deaths.* In text and tables the years around 1870 are often used as reference points; I chose that period, first, to allow a few years for the system to get established and second, to eliminate the special problems posed by the Civil War. For the middle and even later 1860s it is for example not always possible to distinguish victims of gunshot wounds in military hospitals from those in the civilian population.

The basic table used, in the *Annual Health Report,* usually number VI or VIII, lists all causes of death reported, with a breakdown by sex, age, nativity, and color and an indication whether those buried were nonresidents or inhabitants of the almshouse. It is not, however, cross-referenced; except for the adult/minor distinction by sex, it does not indicate the ages of females, for example, or natives or blacks, as distinct from those in other categories. For one year, 1881, no *Annual Health Report* is available. In compiling averages I have simply omitted that year, except for suicides, since the 1889 report includes a table analyzing all suicides from 1866 through 1889.

The other major problem with the health-office death statistics fortunately does not apply to most violent deaths. The problem is that despite their apparent solidity and all the care employed by the registrars, the elaborate tables published each year were built upon a foundation no stronger than the state of nineteenth-century medicine. However accurate in the aggregate, or as a body count, the figures are wholly untrustworthy as a guide to most specific causes of death from disease. The registration figures had to be compiled from hundreds of individual death certificates transmitted each week. Before 1860 the short form was severely edited so as to list only a relatively few causes; after 1860 the published tables included elaborate subcategories (two pages on cancer alone), so that the list ultimately totaled more than two hundred. But the office still had to find categories for such idiosyncratic entries as "excessive bathing," given by a coroner or doctor. The official classification scheme included a number of categories that are difficult to interpret from this distance, such as "teething" and "mania." Most important, a few large miscellaneous categories served to give a light scientific cover to professional ignorance or indifference; thus "convulsions" and "inanition" took dozens of short lives each year and "old age" hundreds of long ones, while "intemperance" and "neglect" registered moral as much as medical opinion.

With a few exceptions, however, the major and most significant causes of death listed under Class XII, "Violent and Accidental," are easily recognizable; no major changes in either diagnosis or classification were made during the last thirty years of the century. Most drownings, burns, scalds, and maimings presented no diagnostic problems; accidents that did, along with the special cases of suicide and homicide, are discussed in the text. Most accidental or violent deaths required a viewing of the body by the elected county coroner, whose office was critical to the compilation of the figures, especially those in which human responsibility was at issue.

The Office of Coroner

The coroner is, next to sheriff and justice of the peace, the oldest of the Anglo-American county offices and remains the least studied. But some understanding of its formal and informal functions is necessary to an understanding of certain indices of violent death. It was the duty of Philadelphia's coroners to investigate all sudden, violent, or possibly suspicious deaths and, if circumstances warranted, to hold an inquest, eliciting medical and other testimony to determine the cause officially. The Registration Act of 1860 declared in effect that all deaths not attended by a licensed physician were suspect and thus required that the coroner be notified. The office was also responsible for the disposition of unclaimed bodies and thus for overseeing the paupers' graveyard. In the case of unidentified bodies, descriptions were issued to the press, rather like lost and found advertisements. Prior to 1870, corpses were stored in the Pennsylvania Hospital; after that year the coroner maintained a morgue.[6]

The job was not inherently attractive. Eighteen men held it between 1839 and 1901, but until the middle of the 1880s only one served more than a single three-year term.[7] One coroner had been a practicing attorney before election, and four were doctors; most came from and returned to the ranks of small shopkeepers. Only one held political office, that of deputy sheriff, before being elected coroner, and only one achieved political prominence afterward. The exception, Samuel Ashbridge, abandoned a career as a coal dealer to become deputy coroner in 1883 and coroner in 1887; he served until 1900, when he was elected, improbably, mayor of the city. In this post he won a modest notoriety as the most clownish of the Philadelphia officials chronicled by Lincoln Steffens in *The Shame of the Cities*.[8]

Ashbridge's career was exceptional, but there is little to indicate high purpose or ability among most of his predecessors, and if not rich in opportunities for the petty grafting that generally characterized urban government, the office was not wholly lacking, either. During the term of Samuel Heintzleman in 1840, there were allegations that the dollar a day paid to inquest jurors was being siphoned off at some point, and that the whole business was becoming inordinately expensive. Some 1,088 inquests were held between October 1836 and January 1840, with $2.75 paid to the coroner each time, a total expense to the county of $13,064.[9] Heintzleman further aroused civic indignation by holding full inquests, "in violation of law and tradition," over routine stillbirths and cases of "apoplexy."[10] In 1845 the state passed a special law for Philadelphia that reduced the number of jurors from twelve to six and required that no inquests be held unless a preliminary coroner's viewing suggested something clearly violent or suspicious.[11]

That law remained in effect for the rest of the century, with minor amendments and provisions for growth in the office.[12] As time passed, the size of the city and the lethal effects of industrialism made it unnecessary for its occupant to scrabble for business. Originally only the mayor and aldermen, who also served as part of the criminal justice system, were allowed to substitute when the coroner was unavailable; later the office acquired its own deputies, as well as a doctor and eventually a detective. In 1876 the coroner himself was granted a basic $6000 salary. Many routine cases, still, were farmed out or "waived" to ordinary private physicians. The law of 1845 cut down but not out the modest patronage that sometimes occurred in hiring favored jurors; unlike trial jurors, those who attended inquests were not subject to elaborate selection procedures. Although a coroner's jury was supposed to be convened on the spot where the body was discovered and chosen from among neighboring citizens, locations such as police stations, hospitals, and the morgue yielded a number of familiar names.

The nature of the office and of the officeholders suggests that certain sorts of verdicts should be carefully examined; each of these is dealt with in the text. But the heart of the system remained intact throughout; the fee system assured that all violent deaths would be noted, so far as vigilance could assure, and that they would be recorded as violent.

One administrative failing, however, especially annoying to a historian, went uncorrected. As an elected official responsible to no other authority, the coroner was not required to keep records except for the collection of fees and the forwarding of docket verdicts to the Court of Quarter Sessions. The verdicts given to the clerk of courts have not survived. Only four sets of manuscript sources still exist, all kept by the Philadelphia City Records Department. Three are cited as Mss. *Coroner's Docket*

Book, with date. From October 1854 through October 1857, Coroner Joseph Delaveau kept careful record of all inquests, listing victims, jurors, witnesses, verdicts, and, beginning in 1856, fees charged to the county. There are two volumes in this series with some overlap—the first is more slapdash, is in a different hand, and does not contain the fees. Dr. W. Kent Gilbert and his immediate successor Thomas J. Powers kept the same sort of book, also in two volumes and with the same information recorded except for fees; this series runs from January 1879 through October 1880. For the first quarter of 1885 there is a volume written under the auspices of Thomas Powers, but in the utterly illegible hand of the then-novice deputy Samuel Ashbridge; a few notes from doctors, pasted in, make it something better than useless. More colorful, although less broadly useful, is a book in which Dr. Kingston Goddard recorded all inquest testimony offered in cases of suspected homicide between March 1875 and December 1877; it is cited as *Coroner's Evidence Book*. All of these manuscript sources taken together give some insight into the working of the office, and allow cross-checking with newspapers, health office records, and other sources.

For the actual mechanics of the trade, later in the century, there are two valuable contemporary works by John G. Lee, M.D., who served for over a decade as the coroner's physician. The title of the first is fully self-explanatory: *A Handbook for Coroners, Containing a Digest of All the Laws in the Thirty-Eight States of the Union, together with a Historical Resumé from the Earliest Period to the Present Time, a Guide to the Physician in Post-Mortem Examinations, and Valuable Miscellaneous Matter Never Before Collated* (Philadelphia, 1881). A man of good sense above all, the doctor reprints the simple rules advocated by a pioneering French pathologist, and while not absolutely endorsing the need for a stiff drink before beginning work on an aging case, he does insist on an empty stomach and adequate ventilation. Dr. Lee also supports one basic contention of this book; in two papers, delivered at different times but collected in one pamphlet, "Homicide and Suicide in the City and County of Philadelphia, Pa., during a Decade, 1871 to 1881 Inclusive" (Philadelphia, n.d.), he points out that over the period covered the incidence of homicide was falling and suicide, rising.

In addition to the manuscript sources cited above, there is, finally, another and quantitatively most important source of coroner's records. From 1874 through 1898, except for 1876, 1877, 1881, 1883, and 1887, the coroners published their returns as part of the *Annual Health Report*. Two others of the same general form were published in the *Public Ledger* but not in the *Annual Health Report*, one for 1899 on Jan. 1, 1900, one for 1900 on Jan. 4, 1901; none appears anywhere for 1901. All of these, cited as *Coroner's Annual Report*, contain a breakdown of the year's work. In 1874 and 1875 this is simply a list of causes of death. The others also report on the number "waived" to private doctors, and the number of whites, blacks, males, females, adults, and minors whose deaths were investigated, with railroad killings listed by company, and suicides and sometimes homicides by means employed.

For any given cause of death the totals from the health office are in most cases slightly different from those published by the coroner. One reason is that some accident cases were neither suspicious nor sudden; a burn victim who died in a hospital under doctor's care, some time after the event and with no doubt as to agency, might be waived. The other is that the coroner investigated all relevant deaths that occurred in the county, whether the person was a Philadelphian or a stranger; the health officer recorded all who were buried in the city's jurisdiction, including a handful of nonresidents and a few residents who died out of town. The coroner, moreover, counted totals by calendar year, the health office by end-of-week interment reports during the year. Unless otherwise specified, all totals in the text are taken from the health office figures. However, in the discussion of suicide some analysis of means is taken from the coroner's figures and some from the health office in order to get a fuller set of data covering more years.

The Census of the United States

For those figures given as rates per 100,000 of population, the population totals are taken from three different sources. The first is the published United States Census for the several census years between 1840 and 1900. The second is the *Annual Health Reports*, described above, which give official registration estimates for every year beginning in 1861; those for the noncensus years between 1840 and 1860 are extrapolated, using standard statistical techniques. A third source is a series of computer printouts provided by the staff of the Philadelphia Social History Project, under the direction of Professor Theodore Hershberg of the University of Pennsylvania; employees of the project have calculated the age structure of each of Philadelphia's principal ethnic groups from the manuscript census reports of 1850, 1860, 1870, and 1880. As with the figures drawn from the health department and coroner's office, footnote references to these sources are generally omitted throughout the text.

The use of seven-year intervals in several tables was dictated by the desire to stress rather considerable long-term changes in rates of death as distinct from short-term fluctuations. In each case the rates were obtained simply by dividing the seven-year totals of some particular cause of death, as suicide or drowning, by the population totals of the same seven years and expressing the result per 100,000.

In addition, it is possible and desirable to present some death rates for some years not as "crude" rates, as obtained in the manner described above, but as "standardized" or "age-adjusted" rates. This is desirable when comparing two or more different populations, such as laborers and professionals, or the Philadelphians of 1870 and the Philadelphians of 1900, which have different age structures, that is, different proportions of persons aged from birth to four years, five to nine, ten to fourteen, and so on. Since violent death rates vary markedly by age—older people being more susceptible to suicide; young ones, to burns and scalds; teen-agers and young adults, to drowning—a fair comparison requires calculating what the death rates of the different populations would be if both the age structures were identical. This technique is possible only when the deaths from a given cause are listed by age categories: so many for persons from birth to four, so many for persons from five to nine, etc.

In Philadelphia, this is possible only for the years after the Registration Act of 1860, and thus the tables involving crude rates for seven-year intervals across the whole period 1839-1901 cannot be standardized.

In practice, the fact that standardization is not possible makes little difference when rates are given for the whole or aggregate population. During the sixty-three years under study, the birth rate, and to a lesser extent perhaps the death rate, was slowly declining, resulting in a gradually older population; on the average, there were over time fewer very young people in proportion to the middle-aged and elderly. But the change was not significant enough to make much difference in aggregate death rates; when it is possible to standardize such rates, the adjustments are never as large as 9 percent and are usually much smaller.

It is possible, however, to make standardized comparisons between the years around 1870 and those around 1900. And in some cases, with groups smaller than the aggregate population, the process does make a significant difference. Although crude rates of suicide were far higher among immigrants than among natives, the native population contained a greater proportion of the very young, since children born to immigrants are counted as native. Thus standardization of the native and immigrant rates by age considerably narrows the gap between them.

In text and tables, unless otherwise noted, the standard age structure used for comparative purposes is that of the population of Philadelphia in 1900, using five-year intervals up to the age of twenty, ten-year intervals thereafter, and treating all persons over seventy as a single category. In all cases the "crude" as well as the standardized rate is given.

APPENDIX B

CRIMINAL INDICTMENTS
ON COMPUTER

Much of the material in chapters 4, 5, and 6 is based upon a study of over 1500 indictments, which includes all those recorded for Philadelphia between 1839 and 1901 in cases of murder, manslaughter, involuntary manslaughter, abortion, concealment of the death of a bastard child, and attempted suicide. These were obtained from the series of manuscript docket books kept by the clerk of the Court of Quarter Sessions. While technically all but the attempted suicide cases were tried in what was in Pennsylvania called the Court of Oyer and Terminer, the same clerk and the same judges, in rotation, served for both. For a period during 1840-1841, a Court of General Sessions was established to deal with the same offenses.

Following the commonwealth's case number, by month, these dockets always list the name of the accused, the charges, and in a homicide case for which a true bill was found, usually the name of the victim. After this there is an indication of the grand jury's disposition of the case, either "true bill" or "ignoramus." If the case went to verdict, the entry also lists, with some exceptions and omissions: the date of arraignment; the plea, the date and nature of any changes in charge or plea; the date of the opening of the trial; the names of the jurors called, challenged, and impaneled; the date and nature of all legal maneuvers; the date and nature of the verdict; and finally the date and nature of all posttrial legal developments, including appeals, sanity hearings, shifts in place of detention, and, if warranted, execution.

In general, like the rest of the machinery of justice, these dockets improved in quality as the century advanced, with fewer obvious mistakes or omissions. Those for the early years sometimes omit, for example, the disposition of cases that ran beyond the term of a given clerk. There is, however, one area that did not improve. By the 1890s, when reporters and officials had finally learned to spell the common Irish and German surnames, the new wave of immigrants from southern and eastern Europe utterly baffled the best efforts of the clerk of courts. The rough phonetic equivalents on the official records ("DeJackamo") often fail to tally with each other, with accounts in the press, or with the city directory listings, a problem that, if not insurmountable, does slow the pursuit of scholarship.

After the information from the dockets was recorded, the next step in finding out the particulars of each crime was to check key dates in the *Public Ledger* for descriptions of persons and events, which could be done only for cases that came to trial. Some 86 percent of murder cases came to verdict, and the vast majority of murders and manslaughters tried, except for infanticides, were covered in the paper, although sometimes sketchily.

Two issues were pursued not in the press but in the Philadelphia city directories: the occupations of accused and victim, and the number of years (if any) during which either person appeared in the directory. The scheme used in coding occupations was modeled on the one in Stephan Thernstrom, *The Other Bostonians.*

The information noted in the worksheet that my research assistants and I used was patterned roughly after that in Marvin Wolfgang's classic study, *Patterns in Criminal Homicide.* Some of our questions, however, are original, notably those involving ethnicity and length of residence in the city. We could not pursue some of Wolfgang's questions, since the *Ledger* was not a trustworthy source for such information as motive or the presence of alcohol in either victim or killer; after an early trial run, these questions were omitted from the worksheet.

In final form the information transferred to data cards was:

1. Number in the overall series.
2. Year of indictment.
3. Month of indictment.
4. Single or multiple accused. In cases in which more than one person was accused of a killing, only the first three names were coded separately for the relevant variables. There were, however, nineteen cases of murder alone in which more than three persons were indicted. The problems of counting these and other "multiples," and the solutions adopted, are discussed later in this appendix. Generally in homicide cases a separate indictment was issued for each victim, no matter how many were accused; early in the century some indictments listed more than one individual accused of cooperating in the same killing, but separate indictments were later issued for all.
5. Charge: murder, voluntary manslaughter, involuntary manslaughter, abortion, concealment of death of bastard child. Multiple charges, such as murder plus concealment, were coded as the highest. The six cases of attempted suicide were not coded for the computer.
6. Plea: guilty, not guilty, guilty of lesser offense, change of plea to lesser offense.
7. Disposition of bill if no trial: ignoramus, no other entry (as in escape, death, or other), nol-pros, quash. ("No other entry" often indicated one of the latter two and was quite common.)
8. Time between finding of bill and verdict: more or less than ten months.
9. Verdict if guilty: of each charge listed in 5.
10. Verdict if not guilty: same as 9, plus insanity.

11. Sentence: death, insane asylum, more than twelve years in prison, six-to-twelve years, three-to-six, one-to-three, fine, suspended sentence.

12. Race and sex of accused: WM, WF, BM, BF.

13. Race and sex of victim: as in 12.

14. Age of accused and victim if under fifteen: accused, victim, both. Information in the *Public Ledger* about ages of adults was erratic.

15. Occupation of accused: unknown, unskilled, semi-skilled, skilled, low white-collar, high white-collar. See explanation below.

16. Occupation of victim: as in 15.

17. Number of years in which accused is listed in Philadelphia city directory: not found, one year, two to three years, four or more years, unclear. See explanation below.

18. Number of years in which victim is listed in directory: as in 17.

19. Ethnicity of accused: Irish, German, Jewish, Italian, East European, other immigrant. These are estimates, based on surnames; see explanation below.

20. Ethnicity of victim: as in 19.

21. Relationship between victim and accused: married, child-parent, parent-child, siblings, in-laws, other relative.

22. Relationship between victim and accused: same address, different sex, same address, same sex, other acquaintance, strangers.

23. Day of the week on which incident occurred.

24. Month in which incident occurred.

25. Length of time between incident and death of victim: same day, one to seven days, more than seven days.

26. Weapon used: body only, gun, knife or sharp instrument, blunt instrument, drug, other.

27. Place incident occurred: victim's home, accused's home, home of both, saloon, street, work, other.

28. Nature of crime: infanticide, domestic quarrel, other quarrel, brawl, robbery, killing by policeman, killing of

policeman, sex crime, sudden fit, abortion, unclear, other. "Quarrel" is here defined as involving two persons; "brawl," more than two; "sudden fit," an unprovoked, impulsive lashing-out, especially at a stranger.

29. Accessory and number.
30. Codefendant and number.

At the bottom of each worksheet, in addition, there is space for a brief description of events, information that could not be transferred to the computer.

Inevitably, some of the information gathered was not used. Question 8, for example, was designed to bring out an apparent relationship between court delays and eventual acquittal, which did not prove relevant to the text as it developed. As explained in the text, little information is available about abortion, beyond the bare trial outcome and what can be learned from the names. A handful of the homicide cases, even, were not found in the press, apparently because of errors in the dates given in the dockets; my research assistants were instructed to look at nearby and likely dates and then ignore such cases. The *Ledger*, finally, did not always yield all the information sought for cases that it did cover; the series certainly cannot match the precision and completeness of a modern study such as Wolfgang's, in which the information was obtained directly from the police. Unless otherwise noted, a figure given as a percentage is the percentage of cases in which the information (for example, about weapon used) was available. For murder, in all but a few cases it was possible to get all the data except ethnicity, occupation, and years in which accused and victim were listed in the directories. Some of the information gathered, however, is inherently less than trustworthy: the distinction between acquaintance and stranger, which was not always made clear in the press, or that between "quarrel" and "sudden fit."

It should be noted that in the several tables analyzing homicides, this offense has been counted in several different ways, each of which is noted in the text or a citation. The problem arises from the fact that more than one person, often three or four, and once as many as fourteen, might be indicted for killing a single individual. More rarely a single person was indicted for killing two, or in one case, nine, people at once. Thus when the *incidence* of homicide was the most relevant information, I counted the number of murderous *episodes*, no matter how many were accused or killed, as in Tables 8 and 13. When the most relevant information was the disposition of cases, as in Tables 10, 11, and 12, I counted the number of indicted individuals, but in order to avoid having the results distorted by the few cases involving large numbers, no more than three individuals were counted per episode. Only twice, in chapter 5, was the actual total of accused murderers counted. One instance required estimating the ethnicity of persons accused, which as explained below necessitated manual recalculation of the computer results. In the other instance, in order to compare the figure with the most relevant modern equivalent, which is the number of persons arrested, the actual number of indictees was calculated, but then only for first-degree murder cases and twenty-one other episodes of clearly nonaccidental manslaughter.

Most references to statistical, anonymous, or negative information taken directly from the series itself are not individually cited or footnoted in the text; the reader may assume that such references were obtained from my computer printouts.

However, six questions in three areas required rechecking because of special problems, so that this information is only partially available from the printouts; the rest was figured in manually. The final count on ethnicity, based on surnames, was entirely my own, superseding the estimates made by my research assistants. Most important, the items about occupation and years in which persons were listed in the city directories were double-checked carefully. Both of these questions were answered, as explained in the text, from the series of city directories. Because the *Ledger* provided occupational data only erratically, it was decided for the sake of consistency to rely upon the directories alone.

APPENDIX C

NOTES ON SUICIDE:
DURKHEIM AND BEYOND

Despite the extensive literature devoted to suicide, social scientists have not taken full advantage of the rich potential in the kinds of records used for this study. Many sociologists have been misled into unproductive dead ends, and historians, who have only recently begun to exploit the undigested statistics of the nineteenth century, have not yet recognized that suicidal behavior may be one of the all-too-scarce clues to the life and culture of those inarticulate groups whose history increasingly concerns us.

If philosophy may be defined as a series of footnotes to Plato, then it may equally be said that the sociological study of suicide has been largely a series of footnotes to Durkheim. *Suicide* is a brilliant book, and in spite of the suspect statistics on which it is based, many of its observations still hold.[1] Its effect, however, in establishing a kind of classical tradition, has been to focus attention on itself in such a way as to prevent fresh approaches to the subject.

Two suggestions in particular have drawn disproportionate attention from both critics and supporters. The first is the issue of wealth or social status. Durkheim and many older authors, even Henry and Short as late as 1954, all found that suicide was disproportionately associated with the rich and prestigious.[2] Several modern students in America have found to the contrary that it is more marked among the poor and lowly.[3] In their insistence upon consistent generalization, however, competing scholars have overlooked the fact that each may be right for his own time. What has happened is what would occur first to a historian: things have changed. This study suggests that in any case wealth and status are not critical determinants of suicidal behavior; not nearly so important as sex and ethnic culture, they are influential largely as they reflect the nature of socialization through work and education. This may be arguable; what is not is the "democratization" of suicide, the evidence that women, blacks, and young people (among others) have recently become more suicidal than they were in the nineteenth century, while rates among adult white males have declined.

The second inherited problem, which is in some ways related, is the concept of anomic suicide, perhaps the most intriguing idea in *Suicide*. But apart from confusion arising from subsequent redefinitions of the term itself, it has been very difficult to demonstrate. It is related to the issue of status insofar as persons of wealth or position have been thought most vulnerable to, perhaps even most sensitive to, those dramatic vicissitudes that might lead to anomie. Traditionally this matter has been pursued largely through attempts to correlate the incidence of suicide with the business cycle, efforts which, like Keynesian fiscal policy, are more easily applied to the "down" side than the "up."

A more fruitful approach to the question of anomie, at least in theory, might be to examine the effects of immigration to the United States. Surely the experience of transplantation, the passage from one cultural setting to another, virtually defines the word in its original sense. And in fact there has been, for whatever reasons, a strong historical correlation between immigration and suicide.

There are great practical difficulties, however, in measuring the impact of immigration on any given group. What is needed is not simply some measurement of immigrant suicide on this side of the water but also, as a standard, a comparable measure for the other side and indeed for the whole passage. And because suicide was recorded in different ways under two or more registration systems, each of which had its own standards and constraints, the results might differ so greatly as to make statistical comparison misleading.

A better approach might be to focus not on the anomic experience of migration, which defines and rather artificially unites the heterogeneous "immigrant" category, but on the experiences that divide that category. As suggested in chapter 2, centuries of cultural difference, which is to say centuries of history, appear to have a far stronger effect on suicide rates than the short-lived experience of transplantation. The differences among various immigrant groups are much larger than the difference between all immigrants and all natives. While some peoples came from traditions in which self-destruction was apparently more common than among Anglo-Americans, other groups, including some of the largest and most important, had lower suicide rates. Indeed, if all the newcomers had come from Ireland and Italy and none from Germany or Scandinavia, there would apparently be a negative rather than a positive correlation between immigration and suicide.

The United States is in some respects the best place for students even of European history or society to study these group differences. Suicide figures in this country are probably more reliable than those used by Durkheim, and certainly more consistent. He compared various European cultures without allowing for differences in registration systems. But here, whatever the characteristic deficiencies of the coroner and inquest system in a given jurisdiction, all immigrants were equally subject to it, making valid comparisons possible.

The classical sociological approach to suicide does embody one central message of importance to historians: rates of suicide indicate *something* about a society and its constituent parts, and problems of method should not discourage the pursuit of its meanings. Although skepticism about official mislabeling is always in order, moreover, the historical records are for many purposes as good as or better than contemporary ones.

By the late nineteenth century the several studies by Dr. Billings indicated that officially reported suicide rates elsewhere in the urban northeast were roughly as high as in Philadelphia, and as high as the modern rates also.[4] With perhaps one important exception, social pressures should operate to minimize rather than exaggerate these rates, so one may assume that an annual suicide rate of 10 or 12 per 100,000 of population is no less accurate than modern official readings.[5] For earlier times, other jurisdictions, and distinctive subgroups, it may be possible to test the bounds of inaccuracy by using and refining techniques similar to those suggested in chapter 2.

What should make this effort worthwhile is the sharp differences among groups underlying the aggregate nineteenth-century rates. It is still not fully clear what suicide means, only that it does not mean the same thing for all. Mysteries and anomalies abound.[6] But for those concerned with the nature, course, and origin of group differences, the fact that men and women, blacks and whites, and members of differing occupational and ethnic groups were so much more clearly distinguished in the previous century should present opportunities to match the problems.

NOTES

Chapter 1: Introduction

1. On this subject see Morton and Lucia White, *The Intellectual versus the City* (Cambridge: Harvard University Press, 1967).

2. The major sources for the critique sketched in the text are Robert E. Park and Ernest Burgess, *Introduction to the Science of Sociology*, 2nd ed. (Chicago: University of Chicago Press, 1924); Robert E. Park, Ernest Burgess, and Roderick D. McKenzie, *The City* (Chicago: University of Chicago Press, 1925); and Ernest Burgess, ed., *The Urban Community: Selected Papers from the Proceedings of the American Sociological Society* (Chicago: University of Chicago Press, 1926). Cf. Morton and Lucia White's discussion of Park in *Intellectual versus the City*, p. 156. For a fuller version of this argument and critique, see Roger Lane, "Crime and the Industrial Revolution: British and American Views," *Journal of Social History*, 7, no. 3 (Fall 1974), 287-303.

3. Ernest Burgess, "The Growth of the City: An Introduction to a Research Project," in Park, Burgess, and McKenzie, *City*, pp. 46-62.

4. Anselm Strauss, *Images of the American City* (New York: Free Press of Glencoe, 1961), p. 50, argues that violence is one of the two images most frequently associated with the growth of American cities. And it may be noted that whatever the rate at which acts of violence occurred *per 100,000 population*, with growth in size there was an increase in the rate

at which they occurred *in time;* a killing a week in a big city may seem more frightening to those who read the papers than a killing a month in a small city.

5. Samuel Eliot Morison and Henry Steele Commager, *The Growth of the American Republic,* II (New York: Oxford University Press, 1950), 952, 972.

6. Arthur Meier Schlesinger, *The Rise of the City, 1878-1898* (New York: Macmillan, 1933), pp. 114-115; Bessie Pierce, *A History of Chicago,* III (New York: Knopf, 1953), 305; Blake McKelvey, *The Urbanization of America, 1860-1915* (New Brunswick: Rutgers University Press, 1963), pp. 93, 128, 264, all refer to rising crime and community disorganization during the late nineteenth century, although Schlesinger expresses a mild reservation about his source, a newspaper account. It should be noted, however, that British historians never adopted the view that was so common in America; while often fiercely divided over a number of associated issues, virtually all have agreed that the movement from the pre-industrial eighteenth century to the industrial nineteenth was accompanied by a decrease in disorderly behavior. See Lane, "Crime and the Industrial Revolution: British and American Views." For a more recent work on crime in London see also Ted Gurr et al., *The Politics of Crime and Conflict: A Comparative History of Four Cities* (Beverly Hills and London: Sage Publications, 1978), part II.

7. One historian, J. L. Tobias, writing of the British experience in *Crime and Industrial Society in the Nineteenth Century* (New York: Schocken, 1967), p. 267, concludes that the criminal statistics of the period are so bad as to be essentially useless. Modern "labeling theory" similarly discounts the use of criminal statistics as measures of behavior for rather different reasons; see, for example, Ian Taylor, Paul Walton, and Jock Young, *The New Criminology: For a Social Theory of Deviance* (London: Routledge and Kegan Paul, 1973). Eric Monkkonen is willing to use criminal statistics, but only if it is kept firmly in mind that what they measure is not deviant behavior but only official activity; see "Labelling Theory and Crime: A Time Series Analysis," paper presented at the Social Science History Association meeting, October 1977.

8. See Roger Lane, "Crime and Criminal Statistics in Nineteenth Century Massachusetts," *Journal of Social History* (December 1968).

9. The histories from which the composite sketch in the text might be drawn include Oscar Handlin, *Boston's Immigrants: A Study in Acculturation,* rev. ed. (Cambridge: Harvard University Press, 1959); Roger Lane, *Policing the City: Boston, 1822-1885* (Cambridge, Harvard University Press, 1967); James Richardson, *The New York Police: Colonial Times to 1901* (New York: Oxford University Press, 1970); Adrian Cook, *The Armies of the Streets: The New York City Draft Riots of 1863* (Lexington: University Press of Kentucky, 1974); Sam Bass Warner, Jr., *The Private City: Philadelphia in Three Periods of Its Growth* (Philadelphia:

University of Pennsylvania Press, 1968); and Allen F. Davis and Mark Haller, eds., *The Peoples of Philadelphia: A History of Ethnic Groups and Lower-Class Life, 1790-1940* (Philadelphia: Temple University Press, 1973), especially chaps. 1, 3, 4, 5, and 8.

10. Cook, *Armies of the Streets*, p. 209, adds a corollary to this, arguing that a variety of recreational alternatives developed after the Civil War, including spectator sports, helped to provide outlets for the energies of the working class.

11. George Rudé's influential thesis about the nature and purpose of mob activity or riot is reflected in Michael Feldburg, "Urbanization as a Cause of Violence: Philadelphia as a Test Case," and Bruce Laurie, "Fire Companies and Gangs in Southwark: The 1840's," chaps. 3 and 4 in *The Peoples of Philadelphia.*

12. For a description of these sources, see appendixes A and B.

Chapter 2: Suicide

1. Specific citations are omitted in text and tables for all figures derived from the principal sources described in appendixes A and B.

2. For the process of standardization by age, see appendix A. The "crude" rate for 1969-1971 was 12.3 per 100,000; when standardized for the generally younger population of 1900, it becomes 11.1.

3. Virtually all sociological studies have simply assumed the validity of official statistics, or at most deplored without systematically investigating them. On this and other related points, see appendix C and Jack D. Douglas, *The Social Meanings of Suicide* (Princeton: Princeton University Press, 1967), chap. 12.

4. See appendix A as well as discussion to follow. There is one relevant study, J. Maxwell Atkinson, "Societal Reactions to Suicide: The Role of Coroners' Definitions" in Stanley Cohen, *Images of Deviance* (London: Penguin Books, 1971). Atkinson's study, which owes much to Jack Douglas, is limited to modern Britain and assumes that the major difficulty is lapses in medical or psychological detection, rather than cover-up or shame.

5. The two early exceptions are Napoleon P. Leidy and Thomas G. Goldsmith, coroners from 1846 to 1852. During that period the rates dipped once below 2 per 100,000 and twice below 3, the only times when such low rates were approached during the sixty-three years. Such low rates may be suspect and account for the mild anomaly noted in Table 2 for the years in question.

6. For example, the *Public Ledger*, July 24, 1900, reported that a doctor was turned in by an undertaker and then reprimanded by the coroner for either negligence or misrepresentation in the case of an obvious suicide.

7. In this chapter, the five-year period 1868-1872 is on several occasions compared with the three-year period 1899-1901. For 1899-1901 there

were suicides enough to provide significant numbers: 160, 153, and 160; moreover, the health office provided no breakdown by sex and nativity for 1897 and 1898, the only years after 1860 for which this was not done (see appendix A). This precluded using a five-year sample at century's end. For the earlier period, the relative scarcity of suicides suggested the need for a full five years; there were 35, 45, 25, 41, and 48 cases in those years.

8. *Annual Report of the Secretary of Internal Affairs of the Commonwealth of Pennsylvania for the Year Ending June 30, 1900, Part IV: Railroad, Canal, Navigation, Telephone, and Telegraph Companies* (Harrisburg, 1900), pp. xiv-xvi, also casts a cold eye on this contention. See also the discussion of railroad accidents in chapter 3.

9. Means were reported for 1882, 1885, and all years from 1887 on.

10. See note 9, above.

11. The crude rate of death from poisoning for 1959-1961, nationally, was an even 1.0 per 100,000, as given in Albert P. Iskrant and Paul V. Joliet, *Accidents and Homicide* (Cambridge: Harvard University Press, 1968), p. 174. In Philadelphia during 1899-1901 it was 2.5. Much of the difference may well be due to improvements in medical techniques.

12. Emile Durkheim, *Suicide: A Study in Sociology*, trans. John A. Spaulding and George Simpson (Glencoe, Ill.: Free Press, 1951), p. 298.

13. Ibid., bk. 2, chap. 5.

14. For a further discussion of this issue, see appendix C.

15. John S. Billings, *Vital Statistics of Boston and Philadelphia Covering a Period of Six Years Ending May 31, 1890* (Washington, 1895), pp. 260-267. In addition to the study for the census, described in the text, Billings wrote two books with a virtually identical format, covering Washington and Baltimore, published in 1893, and New York and Brooklyn, published in 1894.

16. John S. Billings, *Report on the Vital and Social Statistics of the United States, at the Eleventh Census, 1890: Part I: Analysis and Rate Tables* (Washington, 1896), "Occupations in Relation to Deaths," sec. VII, pp. 61-194. The "registration states" were all those in New England except Maine, plus New York, New Jersey, Delaware, and the District of Columbia. Pennsylvania was not included. In this case age-standardized rates cannot be computed as described in appendix A; the standard population used is all males with listed occupations in the registration states; the age intervals are only those given by Billings: 15-45, 45-65, and over 65. This standard population, in comparison to "all males," excludes those under 15 years, with virtually no suicides, and those who were too sick, too old, or otherwise unable to work, with many.

17. The crude rate recorded for immigrants in 1868-1872 was 12.2 as compared to only 3.5 for natives; in 1899-1901 the immigrant rate was 18, the native, 10.5. As the immigrant group was considerably older than the native, as explained in appendix A, the process of age standardization narrows the gap. A number of persons of unknown nativity were

counted as suicides; these I have divided among the two groups not according to their proportions in the population but according to their proportional rates of suicide.

18. The reason for the probably greater gap is that even if the persons of unknown nativity are divided as described in note 17, it seems likely that the immigrants, especially those who had recently arrived, would more often remain unidentified. The proportion of persons of unknown nativity was higher in the five years around 1870, with 30 cases out of a total of 194, than in the three years around 1900, with 37 cases out of 473.

19. The wards with the highest death rates in 1870, as listed in the *Annual Health Report*, were 1, 2, 4, 5, 7, 11, 12, 15, 17, 18, 19, 24, and 26; 16 fell in the middle. The unhealthiest were 1, 2, 11, 17, 18, and 19; the healthiest were 13, 14, 21, 22, 23, and 27. For 1900, the wards with highest rates were 1, 2, 3, 6, 7, 8, 9, 10, 15, 17, 18, 19, 21, 24, 25, 26, 28, 29, 30, and 40; ward 27, containing the almshouse and St. Vincent's Asylum, is not counted. The unhealthiest five were 1, 7, 8, 10, and 19; the healthiest, 5, 11, 32, 38, and 41.

20. Billings, *Vital Statistics of Boston and Philadelphia*, p. 44, gives the rates of various foreign-born groups for Boston and Philadelphia combined.

21. *Report on Statistics: 1890*, p. 465. In this volume, as in the others supervised by Dr. Billings, the information given is often not quite the information wanted: thus the figures for the birthplaces of the mothers of suicides, rather than those of suicides themselves.

22. A number of demographic and other changes affect a comparison of nineteenth-century with more recent rates of suicide, but the most important of those relevant to Table 4 is the great increase in this century of the proportion of the elderly in the general population. This has the effect of lowering the crude rate of 1969-1971 when the two periods are standardized by age. The crude rates for the later period are 12.3 for the whole population, 15.9 for white males, 10.4 for white females, 13.2 for the white population. See also chapter 6 and appendix C for further discussion of this issue.

23. The contagious effect of suicide news, another of Durkheim's suggestions that is often reconfirmed, was evident in nineteenth-century Philadelphia as well. See appendix C.

24. *Public Ledger*, July 9 and 10, 1841.

25. Ibid., July 30, 1841.

27. A. Alvarez, *The Savage God* (New York: Random House, 1972), pp. 83-85.

27. *Public Ledger*, July 23, 1840.

28. Ibid., Dec. 1, 1840.

Chapter 3: Accident

1. As in the other chapters, specific citations for those materials taken from the sources described in appendixes A and B are omitted.

2. Billings, *Vital Statistics of Boston and Philadelphia*, table 103, pp. 260-267, shows the number of males in Philadelphia, by occupation, who died from accidental and other causes.

3. H. W. Schotter, *The Growth and Development of the Pennsylvania Railroad Company* (Philadelphia: Allen, Lane, & Scott, 1927), pp. 3, 267.

4. Crystal Eastman, *Work-Accidents and the Law* (New York: Russell Sage Foundation, 1910), p. 127.

5. Ibid., pp. 196-200.

6. *Coroner's Docket Books*, 1854-1857.

7. *Coroner's Docket Books*, 1878-1880.

8. *Annual Report of the Secretary of Internal Affairs, Part IV* (1898), p. 506.

9. I am indebted to Professor Harold Cox of Wilkes College for much valuable information about nineteenth-century railroading.

10. Billings, *Vital Statistics of Boston and Philadelphia*, Table 103, p. 267, reports that 126 out of 217, or 58 percent, of railway workers' deaths in Philadelphia between 1885 and 1890 were due to accident; no other occupation was even half as lethal.

11. Pennsylvania's railroads were required to report their accidents, by time, place, nature, and cause, originally to the auditor general, later to the secretary for internal affairs. For proportion of deaths to various classes of people, see *Annual Report of the Secretary of Internal Affairs, Part IV* (1879) and its successors.

12. The calculation is as follows. From 1869 to 1871 accident information was included in the *Annual Report of the Auditor General of the State of Pennsylvania . . . of the Reports of the Railroad, Canal, and Telegraph Companies* (Harrisburg, 1870) and its successors. Although originally every accident was reported by nature, place, and date, later the larger companies offered only statewide totals, without details. For the three years in question, Philadelphia horse cars killed 28, and steam roads exclusive of the Pennsylvania killed 40. The Pennsylvania Railroad's statewide total was 269, but at that time it operated only a single straight route in the city. For 1862 and 1863, the last two years that the Pennsylvania did report individual accidents, only 10 of 110, one-eleventh, occurred in Philadelphia. An appropriate figure for 1869-1871 would be perhaps one-ninth of the 269, or 30, making a total of 98 for all horse and steam roads, or 33 annually.

13. Deaths from automobiles in Philadelphia are recorded annually in *Philadelphia Department of Health Annual Statistical Report* (Philadelphia, 1970) and its successors. Motor vehicle accidents averaged 15.7 per 100,000 in 1969-1971; seventy years earlier, railroad accidents averaged 13.0. While it is impossible to standardize these figures by age, the effect would be to narrow the gap.

14. As mentioned in my preface, I am indebted to a number of people for ad-

vice and assistance in medical matters. But for unraveling the mysteries in the health office categories, the best sources were coroner's verdicts and death certificates; these, unlike old texts or physicians in any age, necessarily had to reduce "causes" to a word or two.

15. Counts obtained from the *Public Ledger* are not inaccurate so far as they go, but it is not clear how far that is, or whether and how it differed between the two years. For the known categories that can be checked with the health office or coroner's returns, it appears that in both periods the paper reported about 90 percent of all instant fatalities, such as drownings—as well as homicides and suicides—and most railroad deaths, but undercounted other types, such as falls, burns and scalds, etc. The only marked difference between 1870 and 1900 in this respect was the greater undercount of burns and scalds in the earlier year.

16. The *Annual Address of the Mayor of Philadelphia* (Philadelphia: 1856) and its successors contain an *Annual Report of the Fire Marshal*, usually separate, sometimes a subsection under the *Annual Report of the Chief of Police*, in the same series. All of these are hereinafter referred to as *Annual Report*, with year covered.

17. The *Annual Report of the Chief Engineer for the Fire Department*, like the fire marshal's report, is not so helpful as it might be. All of these listings are roughly similar, over the last thirty years of the century, but like the health office reports of deaths from natural causes (see appendix A) they contain large miscellaneous categories that preclude any meaningful quantitative analysis. Thus the chief's *Annual Report* for 1900 lists 301 "coal oil lamp" fires, 50 "coal oil stove," 323 "gasoline stove," 224 "gas jet," 86 "electric light wires," but also 189 "child with match," 201 "foul chimney"—type unspecified, 106 "spontaneous combustion," 130 "stove," 281 "match," and 331 "unknown." The total number of alarms was 3,121.

18. Siegfried Gideon, *Mechanization Takes Command: A Contribution to Anonymous History* (New York: Oxford University Press, 1948), pp. 537-539, and Russell Lynes, *The Domesticated Americans* (New York, Harper and Row, 1963), p. 120. For an estimate of the relative lethality of gasoline stoves and electric wiring, see note 17. If "coal oil stove" and "coal oil lamp" are combined and given first place, then two of the four most hazardous sources of domestic technology in the year 1900—electricity and gasoline—were unknown in 1870.

19. Missouri editor of the 1890s, quoted in Lynes, *Domesticated Americans*, p. 120.

20. For rich and poor ward listings, as determined by death rates, see chapter 2, note 19.

21. The crude death rate from drowning for these years was 18.0; the standard population used is that for 1900.

22. Reports of harbor police lieutenants are contained in *Annual Police Report*, by year.

23. According to a newspaper count, 79 percent of the river drownings of 1870 occurred in the Delaware, compared with 72 percent in 1900, when the population had moved west toward the Schuylkill.

24. Ward maps of Philadelphia were published in Philadelphia Bureau of Survey, *A Genealogy of the Wards of Philadelphia* (Philadelphia, 1959). The landlocked wards of 1870 were 12, 13, 14, 17, and 19; those of 1900 were 12, 13, 14, 17, 19, 20, 22, 31, 33, 34, 35, and 37.

25. These figures by wards, although they cannot be standardized by age precisely, are given as prorated fractions of the age-standardized figure for 1869-1871 of 18.5 per 100,000, as compared to the crude rate of 18.0. The difference, clearly, is very slight.

Chapter 4: Homicide: I

1. The sex, ethnicity, and race of accused murderers is discussed in chapter 5, their social class in chapter 6.

2. The Sowers case is not included in the computerized series of homicide indictments made for this study (see appendix B), since the indictment was issued in the last month of 1838 rather than the first of 1839, when the trial was held. The story is however too richly illustrative to omit. The outline in the text comes from the *Public Ledger*, Jan. 4, 15, 16, 19, 21, 23, 25, and 31; Feb. 7 and 11, 1839.

3. The Detriro case is listed in the Docket Book as Commonwealth no. 128 for the December term of 1901. The story is outlined in the *Ledger*, Jan. 30, 1902 (see appendix B). Hereinafter, cases in the series are noted by case number, month and year of term, and date of verdict, as "Com. 128, Dec. 1901, Jan. 1, 1902." The story of the incident may be reconstructed, with references backward and, more rarely, forward, from the account in the *Ledger* following the verdict. Specific reference is made only to those incidents about which specific details, such as names, are given in the text. Newspaper references are given for cases that did not come to verdict and thus cannot be reconstructed as outlined above. When important information was obtained from a source other than the court docket or the *Ledger*, it is cited in the conventional fashion.

4. On the superiority of criminal arrest rates as a source, see Thorstein Sellin and Marvin E. Wolfgang, *The Measurement of Delinquency* (New York: Wiley, 1964), p. 31.

5. *Coroner's Docket Book*, 1879, entry for July 9.

6. *Coroner's Docket Book*, 1885, entry for Dec. 16, 1885.

7. Poisonings in *Coroner's Docket Book* for 1878, Gustlich family, March 6; self-defense, Ibid., 1879, Charles Herman, June 21; obnoxious drunk, Ibid., 1879, Owen McShaung, June 9; stranger, ibid., 1879, "unknown," April 26.

8. Act of 1814, P.L. 352.

9. See appendix B for further information on indictments.

10. Note that this count is of incidents of murder and manslaughter, not number of persons indicted, which is higher, especially for the earlier period. See appendix B.

11. Rox case is Com. no. 7, Nov. 1840, Jan. 2, 1841. Other information about the case, including previous conviction and pardon, is from *Public Ledger*, May 15, 16, 20, and 29, 1839; Jan. 18, 1840.

12. Lee Kennett and James LaVerne Anderson, *The Gun in America: The Origins of a National Dilemma* (Westport and London: Greenwood Press, 1975), pp. 89-90.

13. Ibid., pp. 149-151.

14. Ibid., p. 156.

15. Lane, "Crime and Criminal Statistics."

16. The history of the penal code is outlined in Harry Elmer Barnes, *The Evolution of Penology in Pennsylvania: A Study in American Social History* (Indianapolis: Bobbs-Merrill, 1927), pp. 105 ff. and 185 ff. On homicide, see *A Digest of the Laws of Pennsylvania . . . Originally Compiled by John Purdon, Esq., Eleventh Edition, Revised, with Notes to the Judicial Decisions, By Frederick E. Brightly, Esq., I* (Philadelphia: 1885), 428-429. The quotations in the text are taken from judicial decisions cited; all are from the nineteenth century; although not all were delivered before 1839, they were merely intended to clarify existing law or precedent. Until 1850 the prosecution in homicide cases was handled by the office of the state attorney general, changed by 1850 P.L. 654 to "district attorney." The latter title is used throughout this study. See also *Report of the Commissioners Appointed to Revise the Penal Code of the Commonwealth of Pennsylvania, Jan. 4, 1860* (Harrisburg, 1860), pp. 5-7, 23-26.

17. *Report to Revise the Penal Code*, p. 23.

18. James Q. Wilson, *Thinking about Crime* (New York: Basic Books, 1975), p. 218.

19. *Report to Revise the Penal Code.*

20. Ibid., pp. 5-7. See also chapter 5 of this book, on abortion and infanticide.

21. The accounts of these cases that did not come to trial are in *Public Ledger*, March 8, 1839; April 5, 1839; April 16, 1840; Oct. 27, 1840; March 9, 1841.

22. Quain's case is one of those in which the docket is in error; see appendix B. The case is listed as Com. no. 14, May 1839, and the charges of murder and involuntary manslaughter noted. After the notation that the murder indictment was ignored, there is no other entry. In fact the case was disposed as indicated in the text. *Public Ledger*, April 10 and 11, May 27, 1839; April 2, 1840; June 15, 1841.

23. Docket entry on Force case is reproduced on p. 55.

24. Fisher murder charge is Com. no. 339, Sept. 1870; manslaughter is Com. no. 98, Dec. 1870, Feb. 28, 1871.

25. Walsh and Donnelly are Com. no. 91, Oct. 1870, Oct. 29, 1870.
26. See chapter 5.
27. Berry is Com. no. 826, Oct. 1900, Dec. 11, 1900.
28. Yeager incident in *Public Ledger,* April 25, 1900.
29. Ibid., Aug. 9, 1900.
30. Ibid., Oct. 1 and 4, 1900.
31. The earliest of these cases in the series involved an involuntary manslaughter charge against seven-year-old Joseph Wischman in the killing of Peter Newton, eight, in a bare-fisted battle over a marbles game. The Newton boy may have been weakened by a recent fall down stairs, which apparently helped the jury acquit young Wischman. Com. no. 472, May 1876, Feb. 19, 1877.
32. Lantrell indictments are Com. nos. 366-369, June 1900, Dec. 6, 1900.
33. Gowan is Com. no. 394, June 1900, June 28, 1900.
34. Dougherty is Com. no. 460, June 1900. See *Public Ledger,* June 28 and 29, 1900.
35. Sheils and Sollenburger is Com. no. 416, Sept. 1900, Dec. 6, 1900.
36. Di Genna et al. is Com. nos. 1-27, Sept. 1900, Dec. 7, 1900, and for the manslaughter charges, Com. nos. 136-163, Oct. 1900, Dec. 7, 1900.

Chapter 5: Homicide: II

1. Marvin E. Wolfgang, *Patterns in Criminal Homicide* (New York: John Wiley and Sons, 1966).
2. The police and health statistics on homicide are published in the *Annual Reports* of each department. I have obtained through the office of the court administrator three sets of computer printouts, each several pages long, that trace the disposition of homicide indictments in each of the three years 1969-1971. They are entitled "Common Pleas Court of Philadelphia, Defendant Dispositions: 1969 Dispositions: Most Serious Crime Convicted," and so on. Current attitudes of respect for the privacy of individual defendents prevent tracing individual cases, as is possible in the nineteenth-century records (see appendix B).
3. Professor Hartleroad has allowed me to see and to cite his data, which is based on a 50 percent sample of all homicides investigated by the Philadelphia Police Department between June 1, 1972 and Dec. 30, 1974.
4. Note that this method, while the simplest, contains two kinds of serious distortion. The nineteenth-century figure, like all cumulative or composite figures in this chapter, is obtained by dividing the number of indicted persons by the sum of the population of all years. (In these figures, the number of persons is the actual total indicted rather than either one per episode or limited to a maximum of three, as in all previous tables.) But these nineteenth-century figures are indictments; in the other two periods, the figures are arrests, from Wolfgang, *Homicide,* and from the *Annual Police Reports* for 1969 through 1971. A large number of cases are

"lost" between arrest and indictment. Further, because of the number of nineteenth-century brawls in which two or more were accused of a single murder, and because of gang activity in the late 1960s and 1970s, in both periods the number of arrests is considerably higher than the number of incidents. The effect of this is to exaggerate the nineteenth-century figure somewhat in comparison to 1948-1952, which seems to have had few of these multiple-killer affrays, and to exaggerate the 1969-1971 figure very much in relation to both. The number of homicide victims reported by the health office in the latter period, for example, was not 1,499 but 1,104; calculated in this fashion, the rate per 100,000 was not 25.7 but 18.9.

5. Although the figures in this table for weapons used are reasonably accurate, the figures for time of death are not so precise, particularly those for the previous century. Wolfgang and Hartleroad based their figures on police estimates, which are much more finely calibrated than given here, but the nineteenth-century materials come only from the newspapers and are much more crude. The only figures generally available are for date, not hour, of death, and I have included only those for murder as distinct from manslaughter. The figures as actually gathered are 57 percent dying on *date* of crime, 27 percent more dying within one week, 16 percent dying after one week. Since at least half of all deaths on the date *following* the crime still occurred within twenty-four hours of the incident, I have arbitrarily but conservatively added 10 percent to the 57 percent figure, in order to make it more nearly comparable with those gathered by Wolfgang and Hartleroad.

6. Wolfgang, *Homicide*, p. 286.

7. Ibid., p. 289. Similar rates for other cities are reported on p. 291.

8. Figures compiled from *Annual Police Reports*, 1969-1971. The police figures differ, but not substantially, from those given by the health department.

9. Wolfgang, *Homicide*, p. 301.

10. Common Pleas Court printout, "Defendant Dispositions," 1969-1971. Few students believe that more than a tiny fraction of those convicted of homicide in modern courts are in fact legally innocent—although the fraction haunts us, whatever its size.

11. Wolfgang, *Homicide*, p. 284, refers revealingly to the coroner as "a capable medical examiner"; the actual change to a system with a medical examiner alone was made in 1953.

12. Ibid., pp. 290-294.

13. The nineteenth-century figures for killings of strangers are suspiciously high. Other patterns confirm that the "real" figure was higher than in the mid-twentieth century, but the method of compilation probably exaggerates the difference. Although newspaper accounts state that there was no previous connection between killer and victim, in some cases they may have been previously acquainted in a way that went unnoted since

it had no obvious bearing on the generally irrational motive behind a saloon or street fight.

The figures for 1972-1974 are not included in the table; they are discussed in chapter 6.

14. With respect to domestic violence, the Grand Jury of Philadelphia County in September 1900 stated that fully 5 percent of all criminal cases in the Court of Quarter Sessions, which handled everything except summary offenses such as drunkenness, were cases of wife beating. That would be 18 percent of all assault and battery cases for 1900, in which the 1,024 assaults and batteries, out of 3,663 total court cases, was proportionately lower than in any other census year from 1840 on. The number of all Quarter Sessions cases from July 1, 1899 through June 30, 1900 is given in the *Ledger*, Nov. 7, 1900. The number of assault cases in the court system dropped dramatically in the late 1890s. These incidents, brought to the system directly by complainants with felt problems, were perhaps discouraged by prosecutors increasingly busy with "third-class" offenses such as "selling oleomargarine," or others of recent invention such as "attempting suicide."

15. On the origins of the underworld and of the detective system, see Lane, *Policing the City*, pp. 56-57, 65, 68-69, 142-156.

16. *Annual Police Report*, 1859, lists vagrancy as the most frequent crime for which "detectives" made arrests, followed by intoxication. Later reports outline the work of the detective bureau in unusually full detail, with arrests and the amount and nature of stolen property recovered by each man or team.

17. Ibid., 1898. The detective force was boosted to twenty-one at century's end, but it always remained small, as did the Philadelphia force as a whole. The chief in 1870 complained typically that Philadelphia's ratio of roughly one man to every 1,000 residents was less than that for any other major eastern city, with Baltimore's 1:600 coming closest.

18. Holmes is Com. no. 466, Sept. 1895, Dec. 2, 1895.

19. Mohrman is Com. no. 256, March 1870, Nov. 17, 1870.

20. See appendix B.

21. Wolfgang, *Homicide*, p. 286; the modern situation has been described by Hartleroad.

22. For a single day, July 16, 1880, the *Coroner's Docket Book* lists three boys, two of them twelve and one sixteen, dead of tetanus from separate gunshot accidents occurring on July 14; none appears to have been of French extraction, and by newspaper evidence the death totals around our own national holiday must ordinarily have been higher.

23. Wolfgang, *Homicide*, p. 228; Hartleroad.

24. *Public Ledger*, Oct. 14, 19, and 20, Dec. 12, 1870.

25. *Coroner's Docket Book*, entry for Sept. 5, 1855.

26. *Annual Health Report*, 1873.

27. *Coroner's Docket Book*, Feb. 13, 1857; April 9, 1857; July 24, 1857.

28. *Public Ledger*, May 14 and 15, 1900.
29. Ibid., June 8 and 9, 1900.
30. These deaths are described in the *Ledger* on March 5 and 25, April 5 and 23, June 15, July 23, Oct. 21, and Dec. 28, 1839; Feb. 5, March 4, Nov. 6, 11, and 20, 1840; June 10, July 6, Aug. 27, Sept. 30, and Oct. 12, 1841; March 7, 15, 19, and 28, April 4, 11, 20, and 27, May 10, June 27, July 1, 6, 8, 12, 18, 19, 23, and 27, Aug. 10, Oct. 13 (3 cases), 14, 21, and 27, Nov. 18, and Dec. 7 (2 cases), 1870; Jan. 2, Feb. 5, 8 (2 cases), 14, and 21, March 2, 3, 5, 23 (2 cases), 25, and 30; April 9, 25, and 27, May 3, 9, 14, and 19, June 8, 12, 25, and 26, July 2, 3, 6, 9, and 24, Aug. 9, 14 (2 cases), 25, and 31, Sept. 8, Oct. 1, 11, 15, and 25, Nov. 5 (2 cases), 21, and 26, Dec. 5 and 27, 1900.
31. Act of March 16, 1870, P.L. 40, sec. 1.
32. James C. Mohr, *Abortion in America: The Origins and Evolution of National Policy, 1800-1900* (New York: Oxford University Press, 1978), pp. 83-85. Mohr and other authorities seem to feel that contraception was less important than abortion in this period. Cf. John S. Haller and Robin M. Haller, *The Physician and Sexuality in Victorian America* (New York: Norton, 1974), p. 117.
33. Mohr, *Abortion*.
34. *Report to Revise the Penal Code*, p. 26; cf. *Com. V. Keeper of Prisons*, 2 Ashm., 227.
35. Mohr, *Abortion*, pp. 50, 73-85.
36. Ibid., pp. 77-79.
37. Ibid., chapter 6. The three abortion cases are Com. no. 292, March 1857, May 21, 1857; Com. no. 586, Feb. 1859, May 2, 1859; Com. no. 772, Dec. 1859, Dec. 8, 1860.
38. *Report to Revise the Penal Code*, p. 26 ff. and *passim:* P.L. 404, March 31, 1860, secs. 1 and 2.
39. Haller and Haller, *Sexuality*, pp. 117-118, 216. Mohr, *Abortion*, pp. 18-19 and *passim*, argues that abortion, while clearly dangerous, was no more so than childbirth.
40. On mislabeled abortions see entries in *Coroner's Docket Book* for Julia Fitzgerald, Jan. 25, 1878; Rachel Jackson, Feb. 23, 1878; and Mary A. Turner, March 13, 1879; compare with entries under the same names in *Annual Register of Deaths*.
41. Some of the indictments give the name of the accused and the charge simply as "abortion," and some give the name of the accused and the charge "abortion upon the body of" a specified woman. This apparently means nothing certain, as some of the former and not all of the latter involved adult deaths. The most striking complaint was Com. no. 724, Sept. 1895; the defendant, Morris Freeman, was accused not of performing an abortion but of insisting upon one in the case of a woman whom his son had impregnated.
42. Com. no. 193, April 1885, May 15, 1885.

43. Mohr, *Abortion*, p. 241.
44. Ibid., pp. 95-98. Abortions performed in the earlier stages of pregnancy were cheaper, and commercial preparations, and those who dispensed them, cost relatively little. On the other hand, an operation in late pregnancy might cost a thousand dollars or more.
45. As in other kinds of cases, the number of indictments for fornication and bastardy rose significantly late in the century not, it seems clear, because of greater need but because of a decreasing tolerance for the violent alternatives, or perhaps a greater faith in or access to the system of criminal justice.
46. Act of June 11, 1879, P.L. 142, sec. 7, was modeled upon earlier precedent in this respect.
47. Homer Folks, *The Care of Destitute, Neglected, and Delinquent Children* (New York and London: Macmillan, 1902), pp. 28-29, quotes Dr. Alfred Stilles, in charge of the children's asylum, as saying that they "were sheltered there on their way to the early grave to which most of them were destined," at least until 1883, when children were "farmed out" to families.
48. *Public Ledger*, Sept. 19, 1840.
49. The police reports usually start with a list of arrests for "abandoning infant"; it appears that there was usually no "sentence" except restoration of the child to its mother, or perhaps reprimand when and if the child was sent to the Guardians of the Poor.
50. *Public Ledger*, July 17, 1840.
51. Ibid., Aug. 25 and 26, 1840.
52. Ibid., Jan. 24, 1870.
53. Ibid., July 10 and 11, 1900.
54. Six males were accused in these cases, only one as a principal.
55. *Purdon's Digest* (Philadelphia, 1883), in addition to giving the provisions of 31 March 1860, P.L. 404, sec. 89, provides a history of the statute and of relevant court decisions, upon which the account in the text is based. See also *Report to Revise the Penal Code*, pp. 25-26.
56. As late as the 1920s, Dr. William Travis Howard, Jr., *The Public Health Administration and the Natural History of Disease in Baltimore, Maryland, 1797-1920* (Washington: Carnegie Institution, 1924), p. 501, stated that, "After all when obvious congenital deaths and infections . . . are excluded, most deaths of infants are really due to causes yet unknown, and former generations were not unwise in declining . . . explanations." This was true even among "pathological anatomists as well as clinicians [concerned with] infants coming to autopsy."
57. *Public Ledger*, Nov. 12, 1840.
58. Com. no. 253, Jan. 1900, Jan. 12, 1900.
59. Com. no. 298, March 1868, July 1, 1968.
60. *Report to Revise the Penal Code*, p. 23.
61. *Coroner's Docket Book*, entry for Sept. 30, 1880.

62. Ibid., entry for Dec. 23, 1879.
63. These "unknowns" may be found in the index to the *Annual Register of Deaths* under "U" and traced by page to find their condition, age, sex, and color when those facts were apparent.
64. *Coroner's Docket Book,* final entry, 1879.
65. The figure is supplied by Dr. Robert Siegel of the Philadelphia Medical Examiner's Office.
66. First figure is from Wolfgang, *Homicide,* p. 32, second figure from notes supplied by Hartleroad.
67. Wolfgang, *Homicide,* p. 191, lists five cases of "concealing birth," Hartleroad none.
68. Rita J. Simon in "American Women and Crime," *Annals of the American Academy of Political and Social Science,* 423 (January 1976), 32-46, notes this phenomenon but argues that it has been exaggerated.
69. Wolfgang, *Homicide,* p. 84.
70. The difficulty in measuring Irishness results of course from the fact that so many Irish have names that are also British. Theodore Hershberg, director of the massive Philadelphia Social History project, has noted that three of the ten most common names among the Irish-born in the census of 1880 are Smith (second), Campbell (fifth), and Wilson (eighth). See *Historical Methods Newsletter,* 9, no. 2 (March 1976) and no. 3 (June 1976).
71. Figure supplied in conversation, October 1977, by Dennis Clark, author of *The Irish in Philadelphia: Ten Generations of Urban Experience* (Philadelphia: Temple University Press, 1973).
72. The 23 percent figure is obtained by count from all indictments for murder, using a rigorous definition (no Lanes, Clarks, Smiths) of Irish surnames. The 30 percent figure is my own rough estimate, a rather conservative one; there were as yet few blacks, Jews, or Poles with Irish surnames to offset the Smiths, Wilsons, and Campbells not counted.
73. The 7.5 figure is an undercount in that it involves only those who were identifiably black and not those who were indicted but not tried, nor those about whose cases little or nothing could be found. However, the age structure of the black population, especially toward the end of the century, when there was a heavy concentration of young adults, would tend to push up the rate slightly.
74. Com. no. 698, Dec. 1859, Jan. 20, 1860.
75. Com. no. 30, July 1900. The case was split into three, with verdicts on Sept. 14, Oct. 26, and Nov. 15.
76. Of the 23 persons accused of robbery-murder and brought to verdict, 16 were convicted of first- or second-degree murder.
77. Com. no. 219, 1870, May 27, 1870.
78. W. E. B. DuBois, *The Philadelphia Negro: A Social Study* (New York: 1899), chap. 12.
79. The murder of an unoffending musician from South Philadelphia outside

of Woodcock Hall prompted a major riot at the funeral; *Public Ledger,* June 21, 1870.

80.   DuBois, *Philadelphia Negro,* pp. 320-321.

81.   Com. no. 403, Dec. 1850, May 13, 1851. All were acquitted.

82.   Eugene Genovese, *Roll Jordan Roll: The World the Slaves Made* (New York: Pantheon, 1974), pp. 443-535, and Herbert Gutman, *The Black Family in Slavery and Freedom: 1750-1925* (New York: Pantheon, 1976).

83.   Strong work has been done in this field, notably by Frank Furstenberg, Jr., Theodore Hershberg, and John Modell, "The Origins of the Female-Headed Black Family: The Impact of the Urban Experience," *Journal of Interdisciplinary History,* 6 (Autumn 1975), 211-233; and by Elizabeth Pleck, "The Two-Parent Household: Black Family Structure in Late Nineteenth Century Boston," *Journal of Social History,* 6 (1972), 3-31. But these studies, and Gutman's relatively thin materials on the urban experience, are largely concerned with the issue of female-headed households, which was so dramatized by Daniel P. Moynihan, and had earlier been outlined especially in E. Franklin Frazier, *The Negro Family in the United States* (Chicago: University of Chicago Press, 1939). These all in general demonstrate a pattern considerably more like the dominant white family structure than did Frazier, as well as various adaptive mechanisms peculiar to black families, but they lack the rich qualitative materials of Genovese's and Gutman's studies of rural and slave patterns. In short, whatever they may demonstrate about formal structure they show relatively little about the quality of family life, its special characteristics, its tensions and its triumphs.

84.   DuBois, *Philadelphia Negro,* pp. 70-71, 490-492; Furstenburg et al., "Origins of the Female-Headed Black Family," pp. 228-230.

Chapter 6: Conclusion

1.   See, for example, Paul Bohannon, "Theories of Homicide and Suicide," in *African Homicide and Suicide,* ed. Paul Bohannon (New York: Atheneum, 1967), pp. 3-29.

2.   Andrew F. Henry and James F. Short, Jr., *Suicide and Homicide: Some Economic, Sociological, and Psychological Aspects of Aggression* (New York: Free Press, 1964), pp. 13-19 and *passim.*

3.   Martin Gold, "Suicide, Homicide, and the Socialization of Aggression," *American Journal of Sociology,* 62 (May 1958), 651-661.

4.   Ibid., p. 654; Julian A. Waller, "Accidents and Violent Behavior: Are They Related?" in *Crimes of Violence: A Staff Report Submitted to the National Commission on the Causes and Prevention of Violence, XIII* (Washington: U.S. Government Printing Office, 1969), 1526. Although it is possible that some accidents are in fact suicides, the same might be said of some homicides in which the killer clearly expects punishment, a circumstance that simply confirms the link between the two kinds of de-

structive behavior. The distinction holds generally between the overtly suicidal personality, internally aggressive, and the accident-prone, externally aggressive.

5. See text below and appendix C.
6. Ibid.
7. It is not practicable, for these groups or others, to construct an *actual* suicide-murder ratio; the suicide figures given in chapter 2 and in this chapter are for different areas and years than the homicide figures in chapter 5. The black suicide rate in the previous century, moreover, is too small to permit serious calculation. But it is obvious that if calculable, all of these differences would be very strong.
8. Gold, "Suicide," pp. 654-655.
9. Sheldon Hackney, "Southern Violence," in *Violence in America: Historical and Comparative Perspectives: A Staff Report to the National Commission on the Causes and Prevention of Violence*, II (Washington: U.S. Government Printing Office, 1969), 397, cites studies suggesting that European children exposed to physical punishment do not react as Gold's hypothesis would predict in this respect, and that there is little evidence that the class differences Gold notes are related to parental use of physical or nonphysical discipline.

    It may be noted here that although the familiar frustration-aggression hypothesis fits nicely, the specific psychological mechanisms that incline an individual toward either homicide or suicide are irrelevant for the purposes of this study. "Social learning theory" would explain it just as well. What matters is that the outward manifestations of the two differing personality types are as described and that differing educational experiences—broadly defined—help to create such personality types.
10. The massive study by E. P. Thompson, *The Making of the English Working Class* (London: V. Gollancz, 1963), has no real American equivalent, although Herbert Gutman's introduction to *Work, Culture, and Society in Industrializing America: Essays in American Working Class and Social History* (New York: Knopf, 1976), should inspire some further work. Cf. Lane, "Crime and the Industrial Revolution."
11. Wilbert E. Moore, *Industrial Relations and the Social Order* (New York: Macmillan, 1946), p. 7.
12. It would in fact be tempting to explain the behavioral changes described simply in terms of the decreasing use of alcohol. But while drink is often associated with homicide, it is also associated with suicide; a culture like that of Sweden may have a high rate of liquor consumption, low rate of homicide, and high rate of suicide. Drinking may facilitate either kind of behavior, but it apparently does not in itself determine the choice between them.
13. Perhaps the most relevant book in this connection is Erving Goffman, *Relations in Public: Microstudies in the Public Order* (New York: Basic Books, 1971).

14. Samuel Bowles and Herbert Gintis, *Schooling in Capitalist America: Educational Reform and the Contradictions of Economic Life* (New York: Basic Books, 1976), p. 174.

15. Gold disagrees to some extent with this extension of his analysis, with its emphasis, more common to historians than psychologists, on the importance of experiences well after early childhood. He also suggests, in a letter of April 26, 1978, two other means through which behavior might be shaped by the impact of industrialism. One is individual, the "anticipatory socialization" through which parents teach their children what to expect upon leaving home. The other is statistical, the "selective socialization" through which the chronically recalcitrant are weeded out of school, factory, or office.

16. Gold, "Suicide," pp. 653, 655, 754.

17. Waller, "Accidents and Violent Behavior," p. 1545.

18. Gold, "Suicide," p. 655.

19. The figures quoted are summarized in U.S. Department of Commerce, *Historical Statistics of the United States: Colonial Times to 1957* (Washington: U.S. Government Printing Office, 1960), p. 207.

20. Bowles and Gintis, *Schooling in Capitalist America*, p. 154. A survey of the adoption of public school systems, state by state, is contained in Elwood P. Cubberley, *Public Education in the United States: A Study and Interpretation of American Educational History* (Boston and New York: Houghton Mifflin, 1919), chaps. 5 and 6. Figures for expenditures on formal education, especially public funds, also show that the greatest percentage increase in the nineteenth century occurred between 1860 and 1870, followed by that for 1850-1860. See Albert Fishlow, "Levels of Nineteenth Century American Investment in Education," *Journal of Economic History*, 26, no. 4 (December 1966), 418-436, esp. 420.

21. Laurie, "Fire Companies and Gangs in Southwark," in Davis and Haller, *The Peoples of Philadelphia*, p. 83, points out that "Drinking and competitive sport were primary pastimes of the members. Most of these volunteers came from traditional crafts, such as tailoring, shoemaking, and construction, rather than from more innovative, discipline-oriented enterprises carried on in factories."

22. There seems to be no better single index to this transformation than the oft-cited table, "Industrial Distribution of Gainful Workers: 1820 to 1940," in *Historical Statistics of the United States*, p. 74. It is difficult to assess the impact of four years of Civil War on this phenomenon. The Philadelphia homicide statistics show what is usually shown during wartime: a drop during the fighting, probably in large part the result of the absence of turbulent young men, and a rise just after, the result of dislocation and possibly of aggressive expression encouraged in the army and without approved outlet in civilian life. On the other hand, service in the military may have been for most an education in discipline and control,

helping to prepare men for factory or office work and inclining them toward suicide rather than homicide.

23. For a description of the Billings study, see chapter 2; for the trustworthiness of the aggregate levels cited, see appendix C. The business of age adjustment by occupational groups is complicated. *Report on Statistics: 1890*, pp. 61-194, gives the numbers of all men aged 15-25, 25-45, 45-65, and 65 plus for each occupation in the registration area. But age-specific rates are given only for all males in the area, not for all occupied males. For the calculations, the age-specific rates for all males were prorated in proportion to the differences between the aggregate rates for all males (p. 464) and for all occupied males (p. 470). Crude rates are: professionals 24.8; clerical and official, 19.1; mercantile and trading, 15.5; entertainment, 12.6; personal service, police and military, 28.1; laborers and servants, 16.6; manufacturers and mechanical industries, 16.0; agriculture, transportation and other outdoor occupations, 11.3. The standard population used is all occupied males.

24. The most striking anomaly is provided by the high rates for sailors, a group distinguished from "fishermen and oystermen" principally by the group regimen under which they worked. At 26.6 per 100,000, their rate rivaled that of bankers, brokers, and company officials—but the group is too small to have committed many suicides.

25. The general analysis offered here appears at first to fit laborers less well than any other substantial group. Without more detailed information as to just who they were and what they did and how, the explanation offered is the best possible.

26. See appendix B. Count is of persons as described in text, to a limit of three per case.

27. The source of this information, besides the materials described in appendix B, is table XXXVI, *Statistics of . . . the Tenth Census* (Washington, 1883), I, 894. The method of classification is that employed by Stephan Thernstrom in *The Other Bostonians: Poverty and Progress in the American Metropolis, 1880-1970* (Cambridge: Harvard University Press, 1973), app. B. While there are some difficulties in translating the census materials, which often distinguish between industries without indicating specifically how operations were carried out in those industries, the figures for Philadelphia, as given in the text, are quite similar to those Thernstrom found for Boston in the same year, except for the greater proportion of skilled workers in Boston and semiskilled and service workers in Philadelphia.

28. The actual percentages are: white-collar murderers, 25 percent, male Philadelphians generally in 1880, 32 percent; skilled murderers, 20 percent, Philadelphians 25 percent; semiskilled and service murderers, 37 percent, Philadelphians 27 percent; unskilled murderers, 18 percent, Philadelphians 14 percent. For caveat concerning these figures, see text.

29. Thernstrom, *Other Bostonians*, pp. 285-287.

30. Ibid., p. 283.

31. Figures for the census years 1850 through 1880 were supplied by Henry Williams, research assistant to Theodore Hershberg at the Philadelphia Social History Project, and obtained simply by counting the average number of male names per page in the directories—those of women averaged about 12 percent of the total—multiplying by the number of pages, and dividing by the number of males fifteen years and over listed in the census. The figures for 1840, 1890, and 1900 were compiled by the same method.

32. Thernstrom, *Other Bostonians*, p. 224.

33. The figures concerning the number of years in which accused killers were listed in the directories are even more striking than those presented in Table 19. They are in small part accounted for by the fact that accused murderers tended to be younger than the general population of male adults, and thus some of them, at for example twenty-one years, might be listed in the directory only in the most recent year, even if they were long-time residents. But while the figures for age are not good, as explained in appendix B, there is a distinct impression that nineteenth-century murderers were not typically so young as those of the 1960s and 1970s.

34. DuBois, *Philadelphia Negro*, pp. 101, 329.

35. Ibid., pp. 104-107.

36. Ibid., p. 127.

37. John Dollard, *Caste and Class in a Southern Town*, 3rd ed. (Garden City, N.Y.: Doubleday, 1957), chaps. 13, 14; Charles Silberman, *Criminal Violence: Criminal Justice* (New York: Random House, 1978), chap. 5.

38. The phrase is from Marvin E. Wolfgang and Franco Ferracuti, *The Subculture of Violence: Towards an Integrated Theory in Criminology* (New York: Tavistock Publications, 1967). The origins of such a subculture among American blacks, to the extent that it exists, have not been explored. The West African cultures of the twentieth century do not seem notably violent. Paul Bohannon, "Patterns of Murder and Suicide," in *African Homicide and Suicide*, pp. 230-266, modeled much of his research on Wolfgang's and concludes (p. 286) that "tribal or recently tribal Africa (despite Western intrusion), is still a solid, relatively stable community in which strife is controlled and the course of life is usually predictable and often pleasant." Kenneth Stampp, *The Peculiar Institution: Slavery in the Ante-Bellum South* (New York: Knopf, 1956), p. 335, devotes a single sentence to the observation that "many slaves were extremely aggressive toward each other"; he suggests that a reputation for physical prowess or ferocity was one of the several sources of prestige in slave society, but he emphasizes acts of rebelliousness directed at the master, not at fellow slaves. I know of no study of Southern planta-

tion slavery at its height that suggests homicidal violence was a major problem, and most recent studies stress instead that community order and cohesion were the rule.

39. For national homicide rates see, for example, Fred P. Graham, "A Contemporary History of American Crime," in *Violence in America*, II, 375. Like all such figures, Graham's are a compilation from several scattered local jurisdictions. Studies in individual cities show less "increase" in these years.

40. Ibid., pp. 375-376. The phrase "about 1960" is used because changes in the reporting process make the precise time of upturn uncertain.

41. William Robert Fogel and Stanley M. Engerman, *Time on the Cross: The Economics of American Negro Slavery*, I (Boston: Little, Brown, 1974), 260; Thernstrom, *Other Bostonians*, p. 214.

42. The Philadelphia health department figures cannot be used here because they have not, during the twentieth century, always given suicide figures by both race and sex. National figures are summarized in Morton Kramer et al., *Mental Disorders/Suicide* (Cambridge: Harvard University Press, 1972), pp. 172-227. Again, it must be noted that composite national figures cannot be fully trusted, but they do show a long-term drop among males between 1900 and 1960, and "in the most recent years"—that is, 1958 through 1960—"female rates . . . increased at all ages" (p. 205). Tabular studies of New York City suicides, published in Herbert Hendin, *Black Suicide* (New York: Basic Books, 1969), show a marked increase among blacks between 1940 and 1960. All of these trends appear to have accelerated recently, as shown by the Philadelphia figures cited in the text.

43. While the simple model here cannot account for the rise in adolescent suicide, some of it may be related to occupation and schooling because of the long-delayed entrance into the "real world" characteristic of modern society and the consequent lengthening of the troubled period of adolescence itself.

44. The standard population used as the basis for age adjustment, for both 1949-1951 and 1969-1971, is the entire population of the city in 1950 and 1970, respectively. In the *Annual Health Reports* for the later years, the figures are age-adjusted, but the standard population used, inexplicably, is the U.S. population of 1940, which may distort the results by failing to show that black males had in some sense "surpassed" whites.

45. Hendin, *Black Suicide*, pp. 5-6. The result of this phenomenon in Philadelphia by 1969-1971 was to create an oddly flat set of age-specific rates, since those for black and white males tended to cross each other, a distribution that raises interesting questions about the business of age-adjustment for the two groups.

46. The pattern for the early 1970s comes from the study by Frank Hartleroad described in chapter 5, note 4. His findings indicate that as compared with the years around 1950, only 32 percent of victims were killed

at home, that 86 percent of arrested offenders were male, that only 19 percent of victims and offenders were family relatives, that robbery was a motive in 13 percent of all cases, that 14 percent of all victims were members of youth gangs, and that in the half-sample, 592 people were arrested for 538 killings. Cf. Table 14, and notes.

47. One of the great weaknesses of the Chicago School was its failure to recognize the impact of industrialization in cities. It is significant that Robert Park, in listing urban vocational roles that might have an effect in shaping character, includes a total of sixteen, none of them involving manufacture or large-scale economic activity of any kind. The majority consist of wholly preindustrial types, such as beggars, clairvoyants, and medical quacks, who might as well have been found in Nineveh as Chicago; see *City*, p. 14. More important, in assessing the possible impact of monotonous work, he suggests, not that it might have a conditioning effect, as argued here, but that it would create a kind of backlash: "Where the division of labor has gone so far that—to cite a notorious example—it takes 150 separate operations to make a suit of clothes," he argued typically, "leisure is . . . a restless search for excitement" (p. 117). What he failed to consider, as perhaps too frightening, was that human beings might in some sense internalize the values of the machine.

Appendix A

1. Act of March 11, 1794, Law Book V, 189.
2. Act of March 17, 1806, 4 Smith 303. There is a brief history of the board of health and its powers in Edward Allinson and Boies Penrose, *Philadelphia 1681-1887: A History of Municipal Development* (Philadelphia, 1887), pp. 112-113, 215-218.
3. *Annual Health Report*, 1860, p. 146.
4. Act of March 8, 1860, P.L. 130.
5. *Annual Health Report*, 1864, p. 42.
6. The Pennsylvania Hospital was being used by coroners around 1840, as shown in *Public Ledger*, July 9, 1841; the morgue was built in 1870 (*Public Ledger*, Aug. 6, 1870) and was used until the end of the century.
7. The list of coroners and their preceding and subsequent occupations is obtained from the list of city and county offices and the names of the office holders in the series of Philadelphia city directories.
8. Lincoln Steffens, *The Shame of the Cities* (New York: P. Smith, 1948), pp. 215-218. Steffens implies, however, that Armstrong was not notably corrupt as coroner, but hoped rather to relieve himself of debt and earn a fortune as mayor.
9. *Public Ledger*, Nov. 23 and 25, Jan. 16, 1840.
10. Ibid., Sept. 29, 1841.
11. In addition to the book by Dr. John G. Lee, described in the text, there is a brief history of the office of coroner in Sylvester Stevens and Donald H. Kent, *County Government and Archives in Pennsylvania* (Harris-

burg: Pennsylvania Historical and Museum Commission, 1947), pp. 306-310 (a useful bibliographic guide prepared for the Pennsylvania Historical Survey). Since it refers only to laws that were still in force, however, there is no mention of the special act of April 6, 1845, P.L. 130.

12. Stevens and Kent, *County Government*, pp. 307-308.

Appendix C

1. Most of the considerable critical literature devoted to this single book has concentrated on problems of theory, largely ignoring the suspect reporting procedures that produced the figures on which it is based. Whitney Pope's perceptive *Durkheim's Suicide: A Classic Analyzed* (Chicago: University of Chicago Press, 1976), p. 11, devotes only a few sentences to the problem.

2. Henry and Short, *Suicide and Homicide*, introduction, summarizes this older tradition.

3. Among those who have done empirical studies that seem to show higher suicide rates among people of low status are Warren Breed, "Occupational Mobility and Suicide Among White Males," *American Sociological Review*, 28 (April 1963), 179-188; Michael Lalli and Stanley H. Turner, "Suicide and Homicide: A Comparative Analysis by Race and Occupational Levels," *Journal of Criminal Law, Criminology, and Police Science*, 59 (1968), 191-200; and above all, Ronald Maris, *Social Forces in Urban Suicide* (Homewood, Ill.: Dorsey Press, 1969), p. 123.

4. For the Billings studies, see chapter 2.

5. If the analysis of the coroner's function in chapter 5 is correct, the exception, in which social pressure has the opposite effect, is the minimizing of costly and "useless" homicide findings by labeling killings among marginal groups, such as blacks, as suicide. This was not done in Philadelphia; homicides of blacks typically went through the full treatment provided by the machinery of justice. But this may have happened elsewhere, and black suicide rates would accordingly be listed as higher than they actually were.

6. The most intriguing contemporary anomaly is that provided by the data on black suicide in recent years. A recent paper by Robert Davis, "Black Suicide and the Relational System: Theoretical and Empirical Implications of Communal and Familial Ties," prepared for the Institute for Research on Poverty at the University of Wisconsin-Madison, attempts to use what is basically Durkheim's model and finds it has little explanatory value. Perhaps the much-maligned frustration-aggression hypothesis, along with a uniquely high level of frustration, may explain the fact that black *males*, as noted in chapter 6, now commit suicide at a higher rate than white males, and that, uniquely, the phenomenon peaks during early manhood. No known theory, however, can be stretched to cover the fact that black *females*, by a wide margin, still have the lowest rate of any of the four groups defined by race and sex.

Index